New York State Comprehensive School Counseling Program:

Middle Level Activity Book

© 2004 New York State School Counselor Association

ISBN 9781493608645

All rights reserved. No part of this publication may be reproduced, stored in a retrieval system, or transmitted in any form or by any means, electronic, mechanical, recording or otherwise, without the prior written permission of the author.

Printed in the United States of America.

ACTIVITY BOOK TASK FORCE

Emily Phillips, Ph. D.
Assistant Professor, Counselor Education
State University of New York, College at Oneonta

Christi Smith
School Counselor
Vestal Central Schools
Vestal, New York

Lucinda Steele
School Counselor
Vestal Central Schools
Vestal, New York

Clerical and Editorial Assistance
Amber Haggerty
Graduate Student
State University of New York, College at Oneonta

Courtney Colliton
Graduate Student
State University of New York, College at Oneonta

Charlita Ryan
Secretary
State University of New York, College at Oneonta

NYS Comprehensive School Counseling Program Committee
Carol Dahir Ed.D., Counselor Education, New York Institute of Technology
David Ford, School Counselor, Queensbury High School
Deborah Hardy, School Counseling Department Chair, Irvington High/Middle School
Doug Morrissey, School Counselor, Canajoharie High School

Message from the Editor

This book is designed as a companion text to NYSSCA's New York State Comprehensive School Counseling Program Model (2003). This model is based on American School Counselors' Associations' National Standards for School Counseling Programs (1997) and attends to academic, vocational, and personal/social needs of children in New York State. There are three activity manuals: Elementary, Middle, and Secondary levels.

The following activities were designed to assist with operationalizing these standards. The majority of the lessons were revised from an earlier edition of these manuals. Most lessons are original. Original or cited as best we could as an adaptation from a published source. These lessons have been designed by practicing school counselors, a counselor educator with a school counseling background, and a few graduate students as part of course assignments in counselor education programs. We expect you to photocopy any you can use, and we provided multiple lessons for each objective in order to get you started. Each lesson is cross-referenced to the New York State Learning or ASCA standards. A chart in the back of the book can help you readily access lessons on a particular topic or covering a particular standard.

Without the dedication of the members of the Task Force, and of the other contributors, this book would not be a reality. The tireless efforts of NYSSCA presidents, the endless task of typing, the tremendous effort to code and format this set of manuals is unimaginable. Without the support of our department, students, graduates, secretaries, and practicing school counselors, this project could not have been undertaken. This set is the result of a grass roots effort to improve best practice in the field of school counseling. We hope we have provided a concrete and useful publication that serves as a guideline to operationalizing the national and state standards.

Enjoy this book. Use it as is, or for ideas to launch your own creativity. The best accolade that this project can receive is to see copies of it tattered, with pages falling out of it from overuse. Remember, this is our best effort to align these lessons with national and state standards. You may find that a number of these match a greater number of standards than we considered.

Emily Phillips, Ph.D., N.C.C.
Counselor Education
SUNY College at Oneonta

A Message From The President

The New York State School Counselor Association is honored to release this document and its companion activity manuals. The culmination of many months of work on the part of people from across the state, NYSSCA's activity manuals are the third and final installment in the Association's *New York State Comprehensive School Counseling Program*. Other components of this project include the *New York State Comprehensive School Counseling Program* text and the *New York State Comprehensive School Counseling Program Crosswalk* that links the National Standards for School Counseling Programs with the New York State Learning Standards.

Professional school counseling has undergone a significant transformation in the last several years. As the education reform movement has grown in American, school counseling has changed to meet society's new demands. The introduction of the American School Counselor Association's National Standards for School Counseling Programs in the 1990s followed by that association's *National Model for School Counseling Programs* (2003), brought us into the 21st Century as a standards-based, data driven profession accountable for student achievement. The three components of NYSSCA's *New York State Comprehensive School Counseling Program* do the same for school counseling in the Empire State's challenging educational environment.

I hope you will look upon the activities in these pages as a gift from your colleagues around the state. These professionals took the time to share their best practices with all of us for the benefit of students across the state. We all owe them a debt of gratitude. Thanks to their efforts, we've begun to build a library of resources we can all draw upon in our day-to-day work. NYSSCA thanks Dr. Emily Phillips, from SUNY Oneonta, and her colleagues. Without their work, these books would not exist. We also thank Deborah Hardy, of Irvington High School in Westchester County. A long-time leader in our field, Deb has overseen all parts of the *New York State Comprehensive School Counseling Program*. Without her guiding vision, this project would have never seen the light of day.

NYSSCA is the only organization in New York State dedicated to the development of professional school counseling for the benefit of students. As a chartered division of the American School Counselor Association, NYSSCA provides leadership, professional development and resources, like the one in your hand, to practicing school counselors, graduate students, counselor educators, and others interested in the profession. If you're interested in learning more about the Association or getting more involved, visit our website at www.NYSSCA.org. Your involvement can help shape the face of profession!

> Douglas Morrissey
> Canajoharie High School
> NYSSCA President, 2004-2005

Table of Contents

Preface xiii
American School Counselors Associations National Standards for School Counseling Programs xv
New York State Learning Standards xxiii
LESSONS 1
    Lesson 1: Box of Locks 3
    Lesson 2: Qualities I Value! 5
    Lesson 3: Egg – Ceptional Attitudes! 8
    Lesson 4: What We Say About Ourselves! 13
    Lesson 5: Do We Accept Others 15
    Lesson 6: What is Stress? Do I have It? 17
    Lesson 7: My Personal Stress Symptoms 19
    Lesson 8: Healthy Ways of Handling Stress 23
    Lesson 9: Same or Different? 27
    Lesson 10: So Much To Do 31
    Lesson 11: More Freedom 33
    Lesson 12: I Am Lovable and Capable. Or "IALAC" 35
    Lesson 13: Good Choices 36
    Lesson 14: Communication Stoppers 38
    Lesson 15: What is Respect? 40
    Lesson 16: Small Decisions 42
    Lesson 17: What I've Done 45
    Lesson 18: Your Five Best Questions 46
    Lesson 19: Where and When? 48
    Lesson 20: What Do We Like? 50
    Lesson 21: A Few of My Favorite Things – And Why 52
    Lesson 22: Newspaper Hunt 53
    Lesson 23: World of Work Spaceship 54
    Lesson 24: Machines on Mars 56
    Lesson 25: Career Vision 58
    Lesson 26: Ask a Neighbor! 60
    Lesson 27: Family Strength or Family Weakness? 61
    Lesson 28: Who Am I? 64
    Lesson 29: How Do I Look? 65
    Lesson 30: Talk To Yourself 69
    Lesson 31: Choose To Win! 71
    Lesson 32: What is the Healthy Choice? 73

Lesson 33: Dear Gabby 76
Lesson 34: How Are Other People Different? 78
Lesson 35: What Does It Take? 80
Lesson 36: Qualities of Citizenship 82
Lesson 37: I Need A Compliment; How About You? 85
Lesson 38: The Spider Web 88
Lesson 39: More Than a Label 90
Lesson 40: Good or Bad Choices? 92
Lesson 41: Are My Skills Useful? 94
Lesson 42: The Ring of Names! 97
Lesson 43: The Five W's 99
Lesson 44: Why People Like What They Do 101
Lesson 45: Out With the Old – In With the New 103
Lesson 46: Male or Female? 105
Lesson 47: What's In a Name? 107
Lesson 48: I Am Unique – What Makes Me Special? 110
Lesson 49: Your Personality Strengths 113
Lesson 50: Feelings Are Okay! 115
Lesson 51: Different Places – Feeling Different 119
Lesson 52: Pressure 121
Lesson 53: Real Life Situations 123
Lesson 54: Are these Good Things? 125
Lesson 55: I See Some Good Things! 129
Lesson 56: Helping A Friend 131
Lesson 57: What Would I Choose? 133
Lesson 58: What Is In My Future at High School – Part One 135
Lesson 59: What Is My Future at High School – Part Two 137
Lesson 60: A Time Plan! 139
Lesson 61: I Didn't Know That! 141
Lesson 62: Part One – Our Town 142
Lesson 63: Part Two – Our Town 143
Lesson 64: New and Futuristic Careers 144
Lesson 65: Changes in the World of Work 146
Lesson 66: A Business Visitation 147
Lesson 67: Understanding Stress Feelings 151
Lesson 68: Tolerance and Anti-bias: Role Identity 155
Lesson 69: Terms of Tolerance and Anti-bias 159
Lesson 70: Aim for Your Star 161
Lesson 71: Career Zone 165

Lesson 72: Communication 167
　　Lesson 73: Equality 168
Index to Lessons 169

Preface

Standards will remain simply statements of what students should know and be able to do until they are brought to life. Once they are integrated across the comprehensive and developmental school counseling program, the standards take on meaningful importance. School counselors can now better ascertain how the results of focused efforts can contribute to every student's academic, career, and personal-social development and to school improvement. New York State school counselors, under the coordinated and editorial efforts of Emily Philips, Ph.D. have contributed their very best to show us ways of integrating the National Standards across grades K through 12 and connecting the school counseling program to the NYS Academic Learning standards.

Best Practices will:
- Provide replicable activities in a simple step-by-step process;
- Encourage school counselors to identify the ways that they impact the instructional program and contribute to student achievement;
- Promote school counselor leadership, advocacy, collaboration, use of data, and technology.
- Help administrators, teachers, and others understand how the work of school counselors contributes to school improvement and systemic change; and,
- Motivate school counselors to align their work with the ASCA National Standards and the NYSSCA l Model.

When New York State school counselors focus their efforts on the mission of school improvement, they widen educational opportunities for every student and can positively impact student achievement. New York State school counselors are leading the way.

Carol Dahir, Ed.D.
Counselor Education
New York Institute of Technology

American School Counselors Associations
National Standards for School Counseling Programs

Competencies and Indicators

Academic Development
Standard A: *Academic Standard A*: Students will acquire the attitudes, knowledge, and skills that contribute to effective learning in school and across the life span.

A: A1: Improve Academic Self Concept

A: A1 .1: Articulate feelings of competence and confidence as learners
A: A1 .2: Display a positive interest in learning
A: A1 .3: Take pride in work and achievement
A: A1 .4: Accept mistakes as essential to the learning process
A: A1 .5: Identify attitudes which lead to successful learning

A: A2: Acquire Skills for Improving Learning

A: A2 .1: Apply time management and task management skills
A: A2 .2: Demonstrate how effort and persistence positively affect learning
A: A2 .3: Use communication skills to know when and how to ask for help when needed
A: A2 .4: Apply knowledge and learning styles to positively influence school performance
A: A2 .5; Refine study and organizational skills

A: A3: Achieve School Success

A: A3 .1: Take responsibility for their actions
A: A3 .2: Demonstrate the ability to work independently, as well as the ability to work cooperatively with others
A: A3 .3: Develop a broad range of interests and abilities
A: A3 .4: Demonstrate dependability, productivity, and initiative
A: A3 .5: Share knowledge

Standard B: **Students will complete school with the academic preparation essential to choose from a wide range of substantial postsecondary options, including college.**

A: B1: Improve Learning

A: B1 .1: Demonstrate the motivation to achieve individual potential
A: B1 .2: Learn and apply critical thinking skills
A: B1 .3: Apply the study skills necessary for academic success at each level
A: B1 .4: Seek information and support from faculty, staff, family and peers
A: B1 .5: Organize and apply academic information from a variety of sources
A: B1 .6: Use knowledge of learning styles to positively influence school performance
A: B1 .7: Become a self – directed and independent learner

A: B2: Plan to Achieve Goal

A: B2 .1: Establish challenging academic goals to elementary, middle/junior high, and high school
A: B2 .2: Develop an initial four-year plan
A: B2 .3: Update and modify four-year plan
A: B2 .4: Use assessment results in educational planning
A: B2 .5: Develop and implement annual plan of study to maximize academic ability and achievement
A: B2 .6: Apply knowledge of aptitudes and interests to goal setting
A: B2 .7: Use problem solving and decision making skills to assess progress toward educational goals
A: B2 .8: Understand the relationship between classroom performance and success in school
A: B2 .9: Identify post-secondary options consistent with interests, achievement, aptitude, and abilities

Standard C: **Students will understand the relationship of academics to the world of work, and to life at home and in the community**

A: C1: Relate School to life Experiences

A: C1 .1: Demonstrate the ability to balance school, studies, extracurricular activities, leisure time, and family life
A: C1 .2: Seek co – curricular and community experiences to enhance the school experience
A: C1 .3: Understand the relationship between learning and work

A: C1 .4: Demonstrate an understanding of the value of lifelong learning as essential to seeking, obtaining, and maintaining life goals
A: C1 .5: Understand that school success is the preparation to make the transition from student to community member
A: C1 .6: Understand how school success and academic achievement enhance future career and vocational opportunities

Career Development
Standard A: **Students will acquire the skills to investigate the world of work in relation to knowledge of self and to make informed career decisions**

C: A1: Develop Career Awareness

C: A1 .1: Develop skills to locate, evaluate, and interpret career information
C: A1 .2: Learn about the variety of traditional and non – traditional occupations
C: A1 .3: Develop an awareness of personal abilities, skills, interests, and motivations
C: A1 .4: Learn how to interact and work cooperatively in teams
C: A1 .5: Learn to make decisions
C: A1 .6: Learn how to set goals
C: A1 .7: Understand the importance of planning
C: A1 .8: Pursue and develop competency in areas of interest
C: A1 .9: Develop hobbies and vocational interests
C: A1 .10: Balance between work and leisure time

C: A 2: Develop Employment Readiness

C: A2 .1: Acquire employability skills such as working on a team, problem solving and organizational skills
C: A2 .2: Apply job readiness skills to seek employment opportunities
C: A2 .3: Demonstrate knowledge about the changing workplace
C: A2 .4: Learn about the rights and responsibilities of employers and employees
C: A2 .5: Learn to respect individual uniqueness in the workplace
C: A2 .6: Learn how to write a resume
C: A2 .7: Develop a positive attitude toward work and learning
C: A2 .8: Understand the importance of responsibility, dependability, punctuality, integrity, and effort in the workplace
C: A2 .9: Utilize time and task management skills

Standard B: **Students will employ strategies to achieve future career goals with success and satisfaction.**

C: B1: Acquire Career Information

C: B1 .1: Apply decision making skills to career planning, course selection, and career transition
C: B1 .2: Identify personal skills, interests, and abilities and relate them to current career choice
C: B1 .3: Demonstrate knowledge of the career planning process
C: B1 .4: Know the various ways in which occupations can be classified
C: B1 .5: Use research and information resources to obtain career information
C: B1 .6: Learn to use the Internet to access career planning information
C: B1 .7: Describe traditional and nontraditional career choices and how they relate to career choice.
C: B1 .8: Understand how changing economic and societal needs influence employment trends and future training.

C: B2: Identify Career Goals

C: B2 .1: Demonstrate awareness of the education and training needed to achieve career goals
C: B2 .2: Assess and modify their educational plan to support career
C: B2 .3: Select course work that is related to career interests
C: B2 .4: Maintain a career planning portfolio

Standard C: **Students will understand the relationship between personal qualities, education, training, and the world of work**

C: C1: Acquire knowledge to Achieve Career Goals

C: C1 .1: Understand the relationship between educational achievement and career success
C: C1 .2: Explain how work can help to achieve personal success and satisfaction
C: C1. 3: Identify personal preferences and interests which influence career choice and success
C: C1 .4: Understand that the changing workplace requires lifelong learning and acquiring new skills
C: C1 .5: Describe the effect of work on lifestyle
C: C1 .6: Understand the importance of equity and access in career choice
C: C1 .7: Understand that work is an important and satisfying means of personal expression

C: C2: Apply Skills to Achieve Career Goals

C: C2 .1: Demonstrate how interests, abilities and achievement relate to achieving personal, social, educational, and career goals
C: C2 .2: Learn how to use conflict management skills with peers and adults
C: C2 .3: Learn to work cooperatively with others as a team member
C: C2 .4: Apply academic and employment readiness skills in work – based learning situations such as internships, shadowing, and/ or mentoring experiences

Personal Social Development
Standard A: **Students will acquire the knowledge, attitudes, and interpersonal skills to help them understand and respect self and others.**

PS: A1: Acquire Self Knowledge

PS: A1 .1: Develop positive attitudes toward self as a unique and worthy person
PS: A1 .2: Identify values, attitudes and beliefs
PS: A1 .3: Learn the goal setting process
PS: A1 .4: Understand change is a part of growth
PS: A1 .5: Identify and express feelings
PS: A1 .6: Distinguish between appropriate and inappropriate behavior
PS: A1 .7: Recognize personal boundaries, rights, and privacy needs
PS: A1 .8: Understand the need for self – control and how to practice it
PS: A1 .9: Demonstrate cooperative behavior in groups
PS: A1 .10: Identify personal strengths and assets
PS: A1 .11: Identify and discuss changing personal and social roles
PS: A1 .12: Identify and recognize changing family roles

PS: A2: Acquire Interpersonal Skills

PS: A2 .1: Recognize that everyone has rights and responsibilities
PS: A2 .2: Respect alternative points of view
PS: A2 .3: Recognize, accept, respect and appreciate individual differences
PS: A2 .4: Recognize, accept, and appreciate ethnic and cultural diversity
PS: A2 .5: Recognize and respect differences in various family configurations
PS: A2 .6: Use effective communication skills
PS: A2 .7: Know that communication involves speaking, listening, and non – verbal behavior
PS: A2 .8: Learn how to make and keep friends

Standard B: **Students will make decisions, set goals, and take necessary action to achieve goals.**

PS: B1: Self – Knowledge Application

PS: B1 .1: Use decision – making and problem – solving model
PS: B1 .2: Understand consequences of decisions and choices
PS: B1 .3: Identify alternative solutions to a problem
PS: B1 .4: Develop effective coping skills for dealing with problems
PS: B1 .5: Demonstrate when, where, and how to seek help for solving problems and making decisions
PS: B1 .6: Know how to apply conflict resolution skills
PS: B1 .7: Demonstrate a respect and appreciation for individual and cultural differences
PS: B1 .8: Know when peer pressure is influencing a decision
PS: B1 .9: Identify long and short – term goals
PS: B1 .10: Identify alternative ways of achieving goals
PS: B1 .11: Use persistence and perseverance in acquiring knowledge and skills
PS: B1 .12: Develop an action plan to set and achieve realistic goals

Standard C: **Students will understand safety and survival skills.**

PS: C1: Acquire Personal Safety Skills

PS: C1 .1: Demonstrate knowledge of personal information (i.e. telephone number, home address, emergency contact)
PS: C1 .2: Learn about the relationship between rules, laws, safety, and the protection of rights of the individual
PS: C1 .3: Learn about the differences between appropriate and inappropriate physical contact
PS: C1 .4: Demonstrate the ability to set boundaries, rights and personal privacy
PS: C1 .5: Differentiate between situations requiring peer support and situations requiring adult professional help
PS: C1 .6: Identify resource people in the school and community, and know how to seek their help

New York State Comprehensive School Counseling Program

PS: C1 .7: Apply effective problem – solving and decision – making skills to make safe and healthy choices
PS: C1 .8: Learn about the emotional and physical dangers of substance use and abuse
PS: C1 .9: Learn how to cope with peer pressure
PS: C1 .10 Learn techniques for managing stress and conflict
PS: C1 .11 Learn coping skills for managing life events

Legend: A:A-1. 1 = Academic Domain, Standard A, Competency I, and Indicator I.
Reprinted with permission from the American School Counselor Association

New York State Learning Standards

Health, Physical Education, and Family and Consumer Sciences

Standard 1: Personal Health and Fitness
Students will have the necessary knowledge and skills to establish and maintain physical fitness, participate in physical activity, and maintain personal health.

Standard 2: A Safe and Healthy Environment
Students will acquire the knowledge and ability necessary to create and maintain a safe and healthy environment.

Standard 3: Resource Management
Students will understand and be able to manage their personal and community resources.

Mathematics, Science, and Technology

Standard 1: Analysis, Inquiry, and Design
Students will use mathematics analysis, scientific inquiry, and engineering design, as appropriate, to pose questions, seek answers, and develop solutions.

Standard 2: Information Systems
Students will access, generate, process, and transfer information using appropriate technologies.

Standard 3: Mathematics
Students will understand mathematics and become mathematically confident by communicating and reasoning mathematically, by applying mathematics in real world settings, and by solving problems through the integrated study of number systems, geometry, algebra, data analysis, probability, and trigonometry.

Standard 4: Science
Students will understand and apply scientific concepts, principles, and theories pertaining to the physical setting and living environment and recognize the historical development of ideas in science.

Standard 5: Technology
Students will apply technological knowledge and skills to design, construct, use, and evaluate products and systems to satisfy human and environmental needs.

Standard 6: Interconnectedness: Common Themes
Students will understand the relationships and common themes that correct mathematics, science, and technology and apply the themes to these and other areas of learning.

Standard 7: Interdisciplinary Problem Solving
Students will apply the knowledge and thinking skills of mathematics, science, and technology to address real life problems and make informed decisions.

English Language Arts

Standard 1: Language for Information and Understanding
Students will listen, speak, read, and write for information and understanding. As listeners and readers, students will collect data, facts, and ideas; discover relationships, concepts, and generalizations; and use knowledge generated from oral, written, and electronically produced texts. As speakers and writers, they will use oral and written language that follows the accepted conventions of the English language to acquire, interpret, apply, and transmit information.

Standard 2: Language for literary Response and Expression
Students will read and listen to oral, written, and electronically produced texts and performances from American and world literature; relate texts and performances to their own lives; and develop an understanding of the diverse social, historical, and cultural dimensions the texts and performances represent. As speakers and writers, students will use oral and written language that follows the accepted conventions of the English language for self-expression and artistic creation.

Standard 3: Language for Critical Analysis and Evaluation:
Students will listen, speak, read, and write for critical analysis and evaluation. As listeners and readers, students will analyze experiences, ideas, information, and issues presented by others using a variety of established criteria. As speakers and writers, they will use oral and written language that follows the accepted conventions of the English language to present, from a variety of perspectives, their opinions and judgments on experiences, ideas, information, and issues.

Standard 4: Language for Social Interaction:
Students will listen, speak, read, and write for social interaction. Students will use oral and written language that follows the accepted conventions of the English language for effective social communication with a wide variety of people. As readers and listeners, they will use the social communications of others to enrich their understanding of people and their views.

Languages Other Than English

Standard 1: Communication Skills
Students will be able to use a language other than English for communication.

Standard 2: Cultural Understanding
Students will develop cross – cultural skills and understandings.

The Arts

Standard 1: Creating, Performing, and Participating in the Arts
Students will actively engage in the processes that constitute creation and performance in the arts (dance, music, theater, and visual arts) and participate in various roles in the arts.

Standard 2: Knowing and Using Art Materials and Resources
Students will be knowledgeable about and make use of the materials and resources available for participation in the arts in various roles.

Standard 3: Responding to Analyzing Works of Art
Students will respond critically to a variety of works in the arts, connecting the individual work to other works and to other aspects of human endeavor and thought.

Standard 4: Understanding Cultural Contributions of the Arts
Students will develop an understanding of the personal and cultural forces that shape artistic communication and how the arts in turn shape the diverse cultures of past and present society.

Career and Occupational Studies

Standard 1: Career Development
Students will be knowledgeable about the world of work, explore career options, and relate personal skills, aptitudes, and abilities to future career decisions.

Standard 2: Integrated Learning
Students will demonstrate how academic knowledge and skills are applied in the workplace and other settings.

Standard 3a: Universal Foundation Skills
Students will demonstrate mastery of the foundation skills and competencies essential for success in the workplace.

Standard 3b: Career Majors
Students who choose s career major will acquire the career specific technical knowledge / skills necessary to progress toward gainful employment, career advancement and success in post secondary programs.

Social Studies

Standard 1: History of the United States and New York
Student will use a variety of intellectual skills to demonstrate their understanding of major ideas, eras, themes, developments, and turning points in the history of the United States and New York.

Standard 2: World History
Students will use a variety of intellectual skills to demonstrate their understanding of major ideas, eras, themes, developments, and turning points in world history and examine the broad sweep of history from a variety of perspectives.

Standard 3: Geography
Students will use a variety of intellectual skills to demonstrate their understanding of the geography of the interdependent world in which we live – local, national, and global – including the distribution of people, places, and environments over the Earth's surface.

Standard 4: Economics
Students will use a variety of intellectual skills to demonstrate their understanding of how the United States and other societies develop economic systems and associated institutions to allocate scarce resources, how major decisions – making units function in the United States and other national economies, and how an economy solves the scarcity problem through market and non market mechanisms.

Standard 5: Civics, Citizenship, and Government
Students will use a variety of intellectual skills to demonstrate their understanding of the necessity for establishing governments; the governmental system of the United States and other nations; the United States Constitution; the basic civic values of American constitutional democracy; and the roles, rights, and responsibilities of citizenship, including avenues of participation.

LESSONS

New York State Comprehensive School Counseling Program

Lesson 1: Box of Locks

Name: Jessica Cooper

Grade Level: Fifth and Sixth Grades

National Standard:
Academic Standard A: Students will acquire the attitudes, knowledge, and skills that contribute to effective learning in school and across the life span.
Personal Social Standard A: Students will acquire the knowledge, attitudes, and interpersonal skills to help them understand and respect self and others.

NYS Learning Standards: *Health, Physical Education, and Family and Consumer Sciences Standard 3:* Resource Management

Resources: Combination locks (enough for 4-5 locks per classroom), baskets (to hold the locks in), combination numbers on the back of locks, information regarding middle school

Note: This lesson is designed to be done either near the end of elementary school final year or for middle school orientation and is presented here as 3 parts.

Session 1 Lesson plan/procedure:

1. Visit the students' current classroom to start the discussion about middle school. Make these arrangements with elementary teachers.

2. Start with an icebreaker. Ask the students to do a go around the room and answer these two questions: Name one thing really exciting about going to middle school. Name one thing you are nervous about regarding going to the middle school. This gives the counselor a chance to hear their concerns, make connections among the students, and helps you figure out what positives to reinforce. If you are the middle school counselor, it gives you a chance to have students introduce themselves to you. You get to know names and faces before they come to the middle school.

3. Introduce yourself and give them a verbal outline of what is going to happen over the next couple of weeks in regards to touring the middle school or your middle school orientation program.

4. Start the discussion about middle school. (Agendas, bell schedule, when lunch is, what type of specials there are, and whatever else is involved in middle school program.)

5. Question and answer time. Students get an opportunity to ask any questions regarding the middle school.

6. With the closing, tell them you have a gift for their class. They need to share this gift, because as you could tell during the discussion, you have similar fears and excitement about middle school. Reinforce that we need to remember that we are in this together, so you expect that they will help each other out with this gift. Then present the class with a box of combination locks. Show the students how to use them, explain the numbers on the back, (Put the combination lock numbers on the back with a sticker), and remind the students to help each other open the locks, especially the "going past the number one" part.

7. Allow time for students to work in small groups, practicing opening the locks.

Evaluation:
Students will learn to successfully work combination locks.

Session 2 Lesson plan/procedure:

The students come to the middle school for a tour of the building and to meet some key people. Bring one classroom at a time. You give the tour, so you can continue to get to know the students. After the tour, the students sit in a classroom, and meet some of the key people, like the school principal, and the school nurse. Give the students a chance to ask more questions, and they get a review of middle school rules. Close with checking on the box of locks, and the students' progress with them.

Session 3 Lesson plan/procedure:

During the summer, students and their parents/guardians come to the middle school to tour the building and meet their teachers. A presentation is given, school supply list is handed out, and there is time for questions.

New York State Comprehensive School Counseling Program

Lesson 2: Qualities I Value!

Name: Bob Wilkins

Grade Level: 6

National Standard: *Personal/Social Standard A*: Students will acquire the knowledge, attitudes, and interpersonal skills to help them understand and respect self and others.

NYS Learning Standards:
Career Development and Occupational Studies: Standard 1: Career
English Language Arts Standard 4: Language for Social Interaction

Resources: Chart Titled: "Qualities That I Value!"

Lesson plan/procedure:

The leader should make copies of the attached chart before the session. Assemble the group, then distribute copies. Ask the group to look at the list of personal characteristics or qualities in the chart and to think about themselves. They should add any personal characteristics that they value that are not on the list. They should mark through or cross out those qualities on the existing list that they do not value. Give the group some time to think about this activity.

Ask if any students would share qualities that they have added to the list. Ask if anyone has crossed out items on the list. Ask them to share their thoughts.

Once students have lists of qualities they value, they should then think about how often they exhibit these qualities. Suggest a guide to help them think about this activity. If an individual would exhibit the quality of two out of three possible times, suggest that they mark "most of the time." If an individual only exhibits the quality one of three possible times or less, suggest that they mark "not often."

After giving the group some time to think, ask for volunteers to share any new learning. Did anyone learn anything new about himself or herself? Does anyone have qualities that they value that they would like to exhibit more often? Suggest that one idea would be to keep a personal log as a way to track how often they exhibit various qualities.

Evaluation:
Students will display understanding through group discussion.

New York State Comprehensive School Counseling Program

Qualities That I Value

Everyone has personal characteristics they value. There are characteristics in the chart below that some people value. There are some open spaces for you to add characteristics that you consider to be important. Mark whether you possess these qualities most of the time, some of the time, or not often.

Personal Quality	Most of the time	Some of the time	Not Often
Kind			
Tries new things			
Dependable			
Honest			
Works With People			
Timely (To School, Etc,)			
Plans ahead			
Friendly			
Organized			
Accepts criticism of ideas			
Listens to people carefully			
Neat			
Helps others			
Courteous			

Lesson 3: Egg – Ceptional Attitudes!

Name: Christine McBrearty Hulse

Grade Level: 6

National Standards:
Academic Standard A: Students will acquire the attitudes, knowledge, and skills that contribute to effective learning in school and across the life span.
Personal/Social Standard A: Students will acquire the knowledge, attitudes, and interpersonal skills to help them understand and respect self and others.

NYS Learning Standards:
Career Development and Occupational Studies Standard 1: Career Development
English Language Arts Standard 4: Language for Social Interaction

Resources: Plastic eggs (enough so that each student has one), Attitude statements (one for inside each egg), Two large poster board "eggs" (one labeled "Positive," and the other labeled "Negative"), Tape, and a Basket.

Lesson plan/procedure:

Introduction: I have been taking a walk around the school gathering something in my basket. Do you know what I have been gathering? (Attitudes) What is an attitude? *It is your state of mind when you approach a situation – Or how you think about something.* Why is your attitude so important? *Because it affects how you look, what you say, how you feel, and how successful you are. It also affects your friends, your family, and your schoolwork.*

Body of activity: Each of these eggs has an attitude in it (a paper with a statement on it). Crack the egg open and decide if the statement inside reflects a positive attitude or a negative attitude. **Move students into small groups of three or four to discuss statements and confirm the decision.** Tape the identified statements onto 2 egg – shaped poster board charts as they are discussed. Students could show agreement to the label by using thumbs up or thumbs down.

Closure: Award each student an "Egg – Ceptional Attitude Award" for participating in the activity. Leave other "Egg – Ceptional Attitude Awards" for the classroom teacher to give upon seeing an exceptional attitude displayed.

Evaluation:
Students will demonstrate learning by group discussion.

Possible Attitudes

For use with both previous and following activity – make copies and then cut strips.

I ALWAYS FAIL

I CAN READ WELL

I CAN CHEAT ON MY TESTS TO GET BETTER GRADES

I AM WILLING TO TRY NEW THINGS

EVERYTHING I TRY, I NEVER DO WELL

PEOPLE DO NOT LIKE ME

I TRY TO BE FRIENDLY

I DO BETTER IN SCHOOL WHEN I STUDY

I FEEL GOOD ABOUT MYSELF WHEN I DO A JOB WELL

I TRY TO BE ON TIME FOR THINGS

New York State Comprehensive School Counseling Program

I AM ORGANIZED

I AM PROUD OF BEING ORGANIZED

Middle Level Activity Book

Exceptional Attitude Award!

On this special day, this person has been given this award.

Name: _____

Date: _____

Leader Signature: _____

New York State Comprehensive School Counseling Program

Lesson 4: What We Say About Ourselves!

Name: Robert Wilkins

Grade Level: 6

National Standard:
Academic Standard A: Students will acquire the attitudes, knowledge, and skills that contribute to effective learning in school and across a life span.
Personal/Social Standard A: Students will acquire the knowledge, attitudes, and interpersonal skills to help them understand and respect self and others.

NYS Learning Standards:
Career Development and Occupational Studies: Standard 1: Career Development
English Language Arts Standard 4: Language for Social Interaction

Resources: Previous sheet labeled "Possible Attitudes," pencils, paper

Lesson plan/procedure:

Make copies of the previous attachment, which is a list of "attitudes." Cut these into separate pieces. Give one attitude to each member of the group. If you have a larger group, give several students the same attitude sheet.

Ask students to take out a piece of paper and to think about how their actions would be different if they believed what was written on the sheet of paper. *How would they act at home? How would they act at school? How would they act around other people? Would they have as many friends? Would they achieve in the same way at school?* Give the group some time to think about what each writes.

Call the group together to discuss what they wrote. *Would people act differently if they believed what was written? What would be the opposite of what was written? Would people act differently if they believed in the opposite of the sheet?*

Then, ask people to share if they learned anything new with this activity. *Did they learn this from other people or themselves? Would they be willing to share what they have learned? Ask who might be willing to try an experiment where they try the positive version of what the sheet says (either the same or the opposite).* Then ask if they would report back to the group what they have learned. Allow time in the next few weeks for this report

Evaluation:
Students will display understanding through group discussion.

New York State Comprehensive School Counseling Program

Lesson 5: Do We Accept Others

Name: Racquel Jones

Grade Level: Sixth Grade

National Standard: *Personal Social Development Standard A:* Students will acquire the knowledge, attitudes, and interpersonal skills to help them understand and respect self and others.

NYS Learning Standard:
English Language Arts Standard 1: Language for Information and Understanding
English Language Arts Standard 4: Language for Social Interaction

Resources: paper, crayons, pencils, magazines, books, glue, scissors, construction paper, pictures of various people from different cultural background, Stereotype activity sheet.

Lesson plan/procedure:

Note: The following lesson may be completed in two sessions if time allows or can be incorporated into Social Studies or Art.

Students will be given an activity sheet, on which they will have to complete sentence runners. The purpose of the sheet is to help students understand what stereotypes are and how they are embedded in society. They will then be broken into small groups to compare and discuss their answers. Each group will share their answers with the class and the counselor will make a list of all the stereotypes that were brought up in the groups.

The second activity involves the students looking at pictures of people from different cultures. They will guess each person's cultural background and state the reasons for their answer. Students will share the factors they used to determine each person's culture.

In the final activity, the students will be in groups and will be given information on one cultural group. They will use magazines, books, journals and newspaper. They will read the different information that was provided and then list ten facts that they have learned about that group of people.

Discussion Questions:

1. What are stereotypes and how do they affect people's life?
2. Can you think of any events in history that were influenced by stereotypes and biases?
3. How do people learn to make stereotypes?
4. Do you think certain groups are more subject to stereotypes than others? Why?
5. What do you think you can do to help reduce stereotyping?

Evaluation:
Students will make a collage for their particular cultural group. They will cut out pictures that can be associated with that cultural group. The picture might include food, music, famous people, contributions of that culture to society or history, clothes, lifestyle, language, etc. The final product will be a cultural quilt, which will be made out of the different group collages.

The activity sheet will also be given to students as a post assessment of all the information that was discussed and learned over the period of three days. The students will complete the sentences again and compare their answers to see if their opinions and thoughts have changed.

Sample Survey:
Complete the following sentences and then break up into small groups to compare your answers. Discuss any stereotypes that were noticed in your answers.

People on welfare are…

Drugs are used by …

All people who sleep on grates are…

All Jews are…

He is dumb, he must be…

He is smart, he must be…

He likes watermelon, and so does every…

He looks like a terrorist, he must be…

African Americans are…

All Hispanics are…

Women are…

New York State Comprehensive School Counseling Program

Lesson 6: What is Stress? Do I have It?

Name: Shari Forth

Grade Level: 6

National Standard: *Personal/Social Standard C*: Students will understand safety and survival skills.

NYS Learning Standards:
Career Development and Occupational Studies: Standard 1: Career Development
Health, Physical Education, Family and Consumer Sciences Standard 2: A Safe and Healthy Environment

Resources: Chalkboard or Chart Paper; Chalk or Markers

Lesson plan/procedure:

1. Write the word "STRESS" on the chalkboard or chalk paper.

2. Ask the students how many of them have heard of this word.

3. Ask for a definition of "stress." Take all definitions that apply.

4. Explain that stress has three parts to it: behavioral changes, emotional changes, and thoughts/feelings related to stress.

5. Have the students give examples of each of the three areas. Put these on the board or chart paper.

6. Explain that each person has his/her own way of showing stress, and his/her own way of dealing with stress. There are no right/wrong ways to deal with stress, although there definitely are healthy and unhealthy ways of dealing with it.

7. Explain that, for the next few meeting times, the class will be dealing with the topic of stress: identifying it, and learning healthy ways of coping with it.

8. For homework, each student is to interview 2 – 3 adults, asking him or her the following questions:
   When do you have stress?
   How do you know that you have stress?
   What do you do about it?

9. Have several students summarize what they have learned about stress in today's lesson.

Evaluation:
Counselor will assess students' level of understanding based on homework and post activity discussions.

New York State Comprehensive School Counseling Program

Lesson 7: My Personal Stress Symptoms

Name: Shari Forth

Grade Level: 6

National Standard: *Personal/Social Standard C*: Students will understand safety and survival skills.

NYS Standards:
Career Development and Occupational Studies: Standard 1: Career Development
Health, Physical Education, and Family and Consumer Sciences Standard 2: A Safe and Healthy Environment

Resources: Worksheets entitled "My Personal Stress Symptoms," pen or pencil, responses to interviews, chalkboard, chalk

Lesson plan/procedure:

1. Have one or two students review their understandings from the previous lesson (definition of stress, three parts to stress, etc.).
2. Ask the students to take out the responses they received during their interviews on stress.
3. Write the different responses to the three questions on the board.
4. Ask students if they notice anything about the responses. (We are hoping that the students will notice the variety of symptoms and ways of dealing with stress).
5. Explain that, just as every person is unique, so is his/her way of showing and handling stress. There is no right or wrong way, although there are healthy and unhealthy ways of dealing with stress.
6. Explain that, today, we are going to focus on having the students identify their own stress symptoms.
7. Pass out the worksheets entitled "My Personal Stress Symptoms."
8. Have each student check off as many descriptors as they need to describe their own personal stress symptoms.

9. Once this is done, explain again that there are no two papers alike—just as there are no two people alike. Some may show many changes; others, just a few. The next session will focus on being able to identify our stress symptoms, and learning how to deal with them in a healthy manner.
10. Ask students for volunteers to summarize what they know about stress.

Evaluation:
Counselor will assess students' level of understanding based on group discussion.

My Personal Stress Symptoms

Each person develops patterns—physical, behavioral, and emotional—, which can tell him/her that stress exists. We may also identify specific feelings or thoughts that most always go along with the stress we experience. These changes may be obvious to others, but not to ourselves.

Place a check mark next to the symptoms you have during times of stress.

Behavioral Changes:

____Crying

____Being by myself

____Being quick to fight

____Feeling really tired

____Feeling restless

____Not able to sleep well

____Stomach feels jumpy

____Other:

Thoughts and Feelings Related to Stress:

____Thinking I cannot handle it

____Feeling afraid for no good reason

____Worrying about everything, big or small

____Afraid something "BAD" will happen

____Thinking I am worthless

____Thinking that nothing will ever/does ever go right for me

____Boredom

____Unable to concentrate

____Having nightmares

Emotional Changes:

____Sadness

____Guilt

____Depression

____Worried

____Anger

____Grumpy

____Moody

____Scared

New York State Comprehensive School Counseling Program

Lesson 8: Healthy Ways of Handling Stress

Name: Shari Forth

Grade Level: 6

National Standard: *Personal/Social Standard C*: Students will understand safety and survival skills.

NYS Standards: *Career Development and Occupational Studies: Standard 1*: Career Development
Health, Physical Education, and Family and Consumer Sciences Standard 2: A Safe and Healthy Environment

Resources: Sheet entitled "Stress - Breakers," pen/pencil, chalkboard, chalk and a comfortable area for students to lie down (rug, pillows, etc.)

Lesson plan/procedure:

1. Have 2 -3 students summarize what they have learned from the past two sessions.
2. Re – emphasize that every person has his/her own way of dealing with, and showing, stress. There are no right or wrong ways of dealing with stress, but there are definitely healthy and unhealthy ways of dealing with it.
3. Explain to the students that today's lesson will focus on the healthy ways of dealing with stress.
4. Pass out the sheet entitled "Stress - Breakers." Ask the students if they can think of any other ideas to add to the list. Have them write them on the bottom of the page, or on the back.
5. Introduce the idea of relaxation and guided imagery.
6. Have everyone find a comfortable place to lie down. Emphasize that, in order for this to work, the participants must take the activity seriously.
7. Once students have settled, have them close their eyes. Do a relaxation exercise of guided imagery. (One is provided on the next page.)

8. When completed, have students return to their seats for a discussion of thoughts, feelings about the exercise.
9. Have students write down the most important things they have learned during the lessons on stress.

Evaluation:
Counselor will assess students' level of understanding based on activity discussions.

Stress - Breakers

Relaxation and stress – reducing techniques are your first "line of defense" when confronting negative stress, but you should not stop here. There are times when you do not want to use these methods, or you just want to do something different when you feel tense. In these moments, you need to have a second line of defense for managing stress.

This second line of defense involves using "Stress - Breakers." They are simple and comfortable to use and very effective in breaking the stress. Try using several stress – breakers when you need a break from your negative stress. These stress- breakers work well with both children and adults. Include several of these activities in your daily life.

- Enjoy a good laugh, watch a silly TV show, tell a joke, be a little silly yourself.
- Hunt for a four-leaf clover.
- Look for shapes in the clouds.
- Go fishing.
- Go to a relaxing movie.
- Go on a creek walk.
- Take your camera and go find an interesting picture.
- Color, paint, doodle.
- Read.
- Plan a "pretend" vacation.
- Get a back rub.
- Give someone a big hug.
- Call a special friend on the telephone.
- Observe fish swimming in a tank.
- Listen to the rainfall, or to the waves washing up on the shore.
- Have a picnic.
- Take a walk.
- Sing, dance.
- Talk to a friend.
- Write in a journal.
- Play with a family pet.
- Daydream about something wonderful.
- Have a good cry.
- Listen to relaxing music.

RELAXATION SCRIPT

IN DOING THIS, TRY TO MAKE SURE THAT EVERYONE IS ON A RUG, OR HAS A COMFORTABLE SPOT. COMFORT IS KEY.

1. Discuss the importance of relaxation for effective problem or stress management. Explain that it is difficult to make good decisions when one is upset or worried, and that ideas come much more easily when one is feeling relaxed.
2. Direct a progressive relaxation exercise by having students sit or lie in a comfortable position and listen while you read the following script.

Directions: Read the script in a calm, gentle, unhurried voice, pausing between each line. Upon completion, allow students to continue discussion at their own speed. Do not rush this activity, or its benefits will be lost.

1. Concentrate on your breathing.
2. Listen to the sound of your breathing.
3. Coming in…going out…over…and over.
4. Slow your breathing down a little, and listen some more.
5. Make your breaths deeper and deeper…and listen.
6. Now, imagine that you are on a quiet, beautiful beach.
7. It is warm from the sun.
8. No one else is around.
9. You can hear the waves…Gently, they come in…and go out.
10. It is very peaceful…and you are relaxed.
11. Feel your legs on the warm sand…let all of the tension flow from your legs into the sand.
12. Relax your shoulders and arms into the warmth of the sand.
13. All the stress is leaving your body…All you can feel is warmth…and very relaxed.
14. Listen again to the gentle rolling of the waves.
15. Feel the warmth…the peace…the total relaxation.

Allow students to stay in this state for a couple of minutes.

16. Now, slowly open your eyes…come back to class.
17. Slowly, return to your seats.

Questions for discussion:
1. How did you feel before the relaxation exercise? During? After?
2. What does it mean to relax?
3. What are some ways you can relax?
4. How do you think relaxation can help you solve problems more creatively and effectively?

New York State Comprehensive School Counseling Program

Lesson 9: Same or Different?

Name: Robert Wilkins

Grade Level: 6

National Standards:
Personal/Social Standard A: Students will acquire the knowledge, attitudes, and interpersonal skills to help them understand and respect self and others.
Personal/Social Standard B: Students will make decisions, set goals, and take necessary action to achieve goals.

NYS Standards:
Career Development and Occupational Studies: Standard 2: Integrated Learning
English Language Arts Standard 4: Language for Social Interaction

Resources: Chalkboard, paper, pens or pencils

Lesson plan/procedure:

Before the session, make copies of the attached sheet. Once the group is settled, distribute the sheets. Tell them that they will be listening to each other. While they are listening to each other, they will be thinking about things that make the other people in the group either the same or different from the others.

First, ask the group to write down some characteristics about themselves on a sheet of paper. Then, tell them that they can use these sheets to help them when they speak. Ask each person to describe his/her self in a concise manner. Ask them to say some things that they like or dislike to do. Also, ask them how long they have resided in the area.

Instruct the group to listen carefully for things that they find the same or different from themselves. Ask them to record the items on the attached sheet.

After everyone has spoken, ask volunteers to share what they have learned about other people in the group. Ask them to share the things that make others the same or different from themselves.

As the volunteers speak, make certain that they speak with respect about the other person, especially when they are talking about things that are different.

Evaluation:
Students will demonstrate learning by participating in group discussion.

The Same or Different?

As the person tells about his/her self, write down *at least* three things about them that makes them the same as you. Also, write down *at least* three things that make them different from you.

Example:	*The Same*	*Different*
Charlie Brown	*Likes Dogs*	*Plays Football*
	Likes Computers	*New in Town*

Person's Name	The Same	Different
A.	1. 2. 3.	1. 2. 3.
B.	1. 2. 3.	1. 2. 3.
C.	1. 2. 3.	1. 2. 3.
D.	1. 2. 3.	1. 2. 3.
E.	1. 2. 3.	1. 2. 3.
F.	1. 2. 3.	1. 2. 3.
G.	1. 2. 3.	1. 2. 3.

H.	1.	1.
	2.	2.
	3.	3.

I.	1.	1.
	2.	2.
	3.	3.

New York State Comprehensive School Counseling Program

Lesson 10: So Much To Do

Name: Bob Wilkins

Grade Level: 6

National Standards:
Personal/Social Standard A: Students will acquire the knowledge, attitudes, and interpersonal skills to help them understand and respect self and others.
Career Standard A: Students will acquire the skills to investigate the world of work in relation to knowledge of self and to make informed career decisions.

NYS Standards:
Career Development and Occupational Studies: Standard 2: Integrated Learning
Mathematics, Science, and Technology Standard 7: Interdisciplinary Problem Solving

Resources: Chalkboard

Lesson plan/procedure:

Ask the group to describe what a baby has to do. The list could be something like:
1. Sleep
2. Eat

Then ask the group to list the things that they have to do now. The list could be something like:
1. Study
2. Wash dishes
3. Take out the trash
4. Make the bed
5. Clean their room

Closure:
Allow the group time to discuss how they have gained responsibilities since they were babies. Ask them if they would like to go back to being babies. Increased responsibilities have also meant increased control.

When they were babies, they were totally helpless. Would they want to be that helpless again? So, with the increased responsibility comes increased control over their lives.

Evaluation:
Students will gain an understanding about responsibility through group discussion.

Lesson 11: More Freedom

Name: Bob Wilkins

Grade Level: 6

National Standards:
Career Standard A: Students will acquire the skills to investigate the world of work in relation to knowledge of self and to make informed career decisions.
Personal/Social Standard A: Students will acquire the knowledge, attitudes, and the interpersonal skills to help them understand and respect self and others.

NYS Standards:
Career Development and Occupational Studies: Standard 3a: Universal Foundation Skills
Health, Physical Education, and Family and Consumer Sciences Standard 3: Resource Management

Resources: Paper, pencils

Lesson plan/procedure:

Ask the group to take out paper and a pencil. Ask them to make two columns on the paper. Ask them to label the columns "Now" and "Ten Years Ago." Tell them that they need to think of things that they are allowed to do now that they were not able to do ten years ago. This may be a difficult process since some will believe that they do not have any freedom. To help the process, the leader may want to ask some questions.

　　Do they have the opportunity to earn money? If so, did they get to earn money ten years earlier? Do they buy things or pick out things to buy that they would not have done ten years earlier? Are they allowed to spend time at a friend's house? Would they have been able to do this ten years earlier? Do they spend more time on the telephone? Did they spend as much time ten years earlier? Do they get to watch television programs that they were not permitted to watch ten years earlier? Do they have more choice in what they get to eat than ten years earlier?

After the group has spent some time thinking about their two lists, discuss how each item on the list seemed to have a "job" connected to it. For example, they spend time on the telephone. Yet there is a limit to this time where they need to either monitor themselves or their parents monitor for them. They spend time at their friend's house, yet there is a time limit where they either need to monitor themselves or their parents check on them.

Closure:
Allow the group time to discuss how they have gained some freedoms since they were babies. Ask them if they would like to go back to being babies. When they were babies, they were totally helpless. Would they want to be helpless again? But, with increased freedom, there is increased responsibility.

Evaluation: Students will demonstrate learning through group discussion.

New York State Comprehensive School Counseling Program

Lesson 12: I Am Lovable and Capable. Or "IALAC"

Name: Christine McBrearty Hulse

Grade Level: 6

National Standard: *Personal/Social Standard A*: Students will acquire the knowledge, attitudes, and interpersonal skills to help them understand and respect self and others.

NYS Standards: *Career Development and Occupational Studies: Standard 1*: Career Development
Health, Physical Education, and Family and Consumer Sciences Standard 3: Resource Management

Resources: Handout with letters IALAC written in 5 separate sections, spaced evenly apart, pencils, pens

Lesson plan/procedure:

1. Look at the scrambled sign divided into sections. Think about the past week. In each section, write something that someone said or did that tore away or added to your sign. (Please do not use names if this is a group activity.)
2. Write a "+" in front of each statement that helped you feel lovable or capable.
3. Write a "-" in front of each statement that helped you feel unlovable and incapable.
4. Using two different colors, color "-"s one color, and "+"s another color.
5. Look at your finished sign. Does it have more of one color than another? What does this show you? Do you agree that you feel this way? Discuss or write your impressions.

Evaluation:
Students will demonstrate learning by discussing their personal tags and writing a reflection piece.

Lesson 13: Good Choices

Name: Ann Morrone

Grade Level: 6

National Standards:
Academic Standard A: Students will acquire the attitudes, knowledge, and skills that contribute to effective learning in school and across the life span.
Personal/Social Standard B: Students will make decisions, set goals, and take necessary action to achieve goals.

NYS Standards:
Career Development and Occupational Studies: Standard 2: Integrated Learning
Health, Physical Education, and Family and Consumer Sciences Standard 3: Resource Management

Resources: Paper, pencil, chalkboard or overhead

Lesson plan/procedure:
Begin by saying, "We would all like to make choices that are good for us. Sometimes we make choices that may not help us. These choices may hurt us in the end. There are various reasons we make choices."

"We all know it is important to have friends and to feel accepted by our friends. We have all, at times, been afraid we might do something that will damage our friendships. We may even feel pressure to do things to keep our friends."

Divide the class into small groups. Say: "Your group's task is to brainstorm situations where friends might try to pressure you to do something. Think about the times when you have felt pressured, or someone you know felt pressured. Without saying who put pressure on you, list those situations." Report to class. Some suggestions might be:
- To skip school
- To smoke cigarettes
- To take drugs

- To shoplift
- To cheat on a test
- To not change clothes for gym
- To wear extreme clothing or hairstyle

Say, "In your next task, look at the situations. Sometimes you know right away if what a friend suggests is OK. Sometimes you know right away that it is wrong. But, sometimes you have to ask your friend – and yourself – questions to find out if it is OK. In your group, brainstorm some questions to ask your friend and yourself." Report back to class. Some suggestions are:

- **Is it safe? -Is it legal? - Could it hurt me? - Would my parents approve?**
- **What are the consequences? -Would it affect my work in school?**

Evaluation: Counselors will evaluate students' learning by assessing students' discussion.

Lesson 14: Communication Stoppers

Name: Judy Fruiterman

Grade Level: Sixth and Seventh Grades

National Standards: *Personal Social Development Standard A:* Students will acquire the knowledge, attitudes, and interpersonal skills to help them understand and respect self and others.

NYS Learning Standard:
English Language Arts Standard 1: Language for Information and Understanding
English Language Arts Standard 4: Language for Social Interaction
Arts Standard 1: Creating, Performing, and Participating in the Arts

Resources: chalkboard and chalk, or chart paper and magic marker

Lesson plan/procedure:

Write the following list on the board or chart paper for the students to see when they enter the class:
- Interrupting
- Challenging/Accusing/Contradicting
- Dominating
- Judging
- Advising
- Interpreting
- Probing
- Criticizing/Name-calling/Putting-down

Begin the activity by reviewing the meaning of the above words on the list.

Ask students to help you role-play each behavior to see what kind of effect it does have on communication. Invite a volunteer to start a conversation with you. Explain to the student that he or she may talk about anything that comes to mind, and should attempt to continue the conversation as long as possible or until you call time.

As the student begins to speak, respond with one of the communication stoppers from the list. Use appropriate gestures, volume and tone, and make your response as convincing as possible. Continue using examples of that particular communication stopper until either the student gives up talking or the point has been sufficiently made. The rest of the students will be observing this conversation and you may ask them to guess which communication stopper you are using.

After each demonstration, lead a class discussion about the affect of that communication behavior. This exercise is good to use when a group is having difficulty bonding because they are treating each other in a negative manner. Leave the list of communication stoppers on the board and refer to is during group and refer students to it over the next few weeks as reinforcement.

Evaluation:
Students will be able to describe and demonstrate how communication style can negatively affect the listener.

Adapted from:
Dunne, G., Schilling, D., & Cowan, D. (1991). *Impact.* Innerchoice Publishing.

Lesson 15: What is Respect?

Name: Gilda Narvaez

Grade Level: Sixth and Seventh Grades

National Standard:
Personal/Social Standard A: Students will acquire the knowledge, attitudes, and interpersonal skills to help them understand and respect self and others.
Personal/Social Standard B: Students will make decisions, set goals, and take necessary action to achieve goals.

NYS Learning Standard:
English Language Arts Standard 1: Language for Information and Understanding
Arts Standard 1: Creating, Performing, and Participating in the Arts

Resources: Thinking Questions, pen, paper, and a worksheet with illustrations (can be cut out of magazines, etc.) showing respectful and disrespectful interactions.

Lesson plan/procedure:

1. Counselor will ask two students to play a short skit that deals with a student disrespecting the teacher or vice versa.

2. Thinking Questions – These questions will be given to students after the two students performed the skit:

    1. How would you feel if I slammed the door in your face?
    2. How would you feel if I knew that you were in a hurry at the store and I let you go through the line first?
    3. What does respect mean?
    4. What are some of the ways that students show respect for their teacher?
    5. How do you think a teacher feels when the students show respect?
    6. What are some ways a teacher shows respect to his/her students?
    7. How do you think students feel when teachers show them respect?

New York State Comprehensive School Counseling Program

3. The counselor will hand out a worksheet to the students that contain different students respecting and disrespecting. The student must choose which character is showing respect and which is not. The student must place a circle around the character that is showing respect and an X under the character who is not showing respect.

Evaluation:
Counselor will ask students questions to assess whether learning has occurred

Lesson 16: Small Decisions

Name: Bob Wilkins

Grade Level: 6

National Standards:
Academic Standard A: Students will acquire the attitudes, knowledge, and skills that contribute to effective learning in school and across the life span.
Personal/Social Standard B: Students will make decisions, set goals, and take necessary action to achieve goals.

NYS Standards:
Career Development and Occupational Studies: Standard 2: Integrated Learning
Health, Physical Education, and Family and Consumer Sciences Standard 3: Resource Management

Resources: "Small Things To Do" Worksheet, chalkboard

Lesson plan/procedure:

Before the session, make copies of the attached worksheet for all participants. Distribute these to the group. Begin by saying, "We would all like to make choices that are good for us. Sometimes we make small decisions that can help us a great deal. This week, we are going to keep a log of some types of decisions that can have an impact on school performance."

Ask the group to look at the worksheet. Give an example of how a person might make one of the decisions and the possible result of that decision. Explain that students should keep track of whether they make the decisions as shown and to briefly record the result.

At the end of the week, ask for students to discuss the results of their personal "decision log." Ask for volunteers to discuss their personal choices.

As the individuals speak, stress the connection between the decision and the result. Ask if anyone had any particular difficulty in carrying through with a particular choice on the list.

Evaluation:
Ask people to tell if they learned anything new from the activity. List these understandings on the chalkboard as people share their discoveries.

"Small Things To Do"

Sometimes there are small decisions that can have a large impact. For a week, keep track of your decisions that are related to this chart. Record the result of the time/s when you made the decisions listed.

School Decisions	Have You Tried This Action?	Result?
Being on time consistently.		
Keeping assignment pad.		
Listening carefully to directions.		
Volunteering during class.		
Completing and submitting ALL assignments.		
Organizing your work area.		
Organizing your locker.		
Asking for help from teacher or teachers.		
Writing or processing neatly.		
Remembering to "carry through" with things promised.		

Lesson 17: What I've Done

Name: Bob Wilkins

Grade Level: 6

National Standard: *Academic Standard A*: Students will acquire the attitudes, knowledge, and skills that contribute to effective learning in school and across the life span.

NYS Standards:
Career Development and Occupational Studies: Standard 3a: Universal Foundation Skills
English Language Arts Standard 3: Language for Critical Analysis and Evaluation

Resources: Paper and pencils

Lesson plan/procedure:

1. Ask each person in the group to take out paper and a pencil. Ask them to list the things that they have done since they were have been in school. Give examples like: played in the band, sang in the chorus, studied mathematics, played football, played soccer, etc. Next, ask students to place marks next to those things where they felt successful.
2. Conduct a discussion where people are asked to discuss which things they might feel comfortable doing again. Some will say that they would like to play football or perform in the band or something else. Ask the group if they tended to pick things where they felt past success or things where they had net felt success. Most will say that they chose things where they felt past success.

Evaluation:
Ask the group if they have learned anything new from this experience. Discuss how people tend to choose future activities where they have felt past success. It is more difficult to perform in areas where a person has not felt competent.

Lesson 18: Your Five Best Questions

Name: Bob Wilkins

Grade Level: 6

National Standard: *Personal/Social Standard A*: Students will acquire the knowledge, attitudes, and interpersonal skills to help them understand and respect self and others.

NYS Standards:
Career Development and Occupational Studies: Standard 1: Career Development
English Language Arts Standard 1: Language for information and Understanding

Resources: Newsprint, markers, chalkboard

Lesson plan/procedure:

Tell the group that they are going to play a game. First, divide the larger group into two smaller groups by counting off or drawing lots. Then ask each group to pick a "Keeper of the Answers!" **Tell the larger group that the purpose of the game will be to find out as much information as possible by asking exactly five questions**. Each of the two groups will gather and choose their five best questions. Then each group will ask their "Keeper" to answer each of the five questions. Each person in the group will listen carefully to the answers and record information heard at his/her own desk.

The "Keeper of the Answers" will have information about a person. He or she will answer each of the five questions exactly as asked. After the questions, a recorder for the group will record all the data about the person on newsprint. Allow each group to get together and to consult on their questions. Tell the "Keeper of the Answers" that they are to answer exactly any question asked but no more.

After the two groups have consulted on their five best questions, have them sit in two separate areas out of hearing distance of the other group. Allow the two groups time to ask their respective questions, to share their data and to record that combined data on newsprint. After about fifteen minutes, call the two groups together and compare the information gained.

After a winning group is decided based on the amount of information gained, conduct a group discussion.

Evaluation:

Some questions to ask- Which questions seemed to give the most information? If a particular question "bombed," how could it be asked differently? Did some people seem to hear more than others in the group did?

Lesson 19: Where and When?

Name: Bob Wilkins

Grade Level: 6

National Standard: *Academic Standard A*: Students will acquire the attitudes, knowledge, and skills that contribute to effective learning in school and across a life span.

NYS Standards:
Career Development and Occupational Studies: Standard 2: Integrated Learning
Health, Physical Education, and Family and Consumer Sciences Standard 3: Resource Management

Resources: Paper and pencils

Lesson plan/procedure:

Ask each person in the group to create two headings on the top of a piece of paper. The first heading should be titled: "Where I study." The other heading should be titled: "When I study."

Below each heading, each person should list several advantages of the place and time.

Then lead a class discussion where students share where they study along with several reasons why they have chosen that location. There will be many different choices for many different reasons. Focus the discussion on whether the reasons listed help the individual focus on homework. Some reasons for choice of place will involve other reasons besides being a more effective study location. When there is some difference of opinion, ask for a consensus of the class.

Then ask students when they choose to study along with why that choice of time. As with the choices of location, there will be many times listed.

Some choices of study time will be affected by sports practice, theater rehearsal and other activities. As with the choice location, center the discussion on whether the time helps effective study.

Evaluation:
Students will demonstrate their learning based on group discussion.

Lesson 20: What Do We Like?

Name: Bob Wilkins

Grade Level: 6

National Standard: *Academic Standard A*: Students will acquire the attitudes, knowledge, and skills that contribute to effective learning in school and across the life span.

NYS Standards:
Career Development and Occupational Studies: Standard 3a: Universal Foundation Skills
Mathematics, Science, and Technology Standard 6: Interconnectedness: Common Themes

Resources: Paper and pencils/pens for each student

Lesson plan/procedure:

Ask the class to list some activities that they like to do. Then ask them to list some skills that they need to do the things they like. Then ask them to mark the skills on their list where they feel that they can do well.

Example: **Baseball** – Would need to run fast, have good eyesight, be able to catch things well, be able to throw things accurately.

Now ask them to make a separate list of the activities that they avoid. Then ask them to list some skills that they think are needed for these activities. Now ask them to mark the skills on this list that they do well.

Questions to Consider:
1. Did they notice any connection between things they like and things they do well?
2. Did they notice any connection between things they avoid and skills that they do not feel that they have mastered?
3. Are they more interested in things they do well?
4. Is there any connection between doing something a lot and becoming better at doing it?

5. When they avoid doing something, how do they find out whether they are good at doing that activity?

Evaluation:
Students will demonstrate learning by participating in group discussion.

Lesson 21: A Few of My Favorite Things – And Why

Name: Shari Forth

Grade Level: 6

National Standards:
Academic Standard A: Students will acquire the attitudes, knowledge, and skills that contribute to effective learning in school and across a life span.
Personal/Social Standard A: Students will acquire the knowledge, attitudes, and interpersonal skills to help them understand and respect self and others.

NYS Standards:
Career Development and Occupational Studies: Standard 3a: Universal Foundation Skills
Health, Physical Education, and Family and Consumer Sciences Standard 3: Resource Management

Resources: Paper and pencils

Lesson plan/procedure:

1. In column 1, have students list things that they really like to do.
2. In column 2, have the students tell what they must be capable of doing to achieve the things in column 1.
3. In column 3, have the students list things that they do not like to do.
4. In column 4, why do they not like to do those things?
5. Ask the students to discuss the results. Guide students toward discovering the relationship between their interests and their abilities.

Evaluation:
Students will demonstrate their learning by participating in group discussion.

Lesson 22: Newspaper Hunt

Name: Judith J. Karis and Judith Fruiterman

Grade Level: 6

National Standard: *Career Standard A*: Students will acquire the skills to investigate the world of work in relation to knowledge of self and to make informed career decisions.

NYS Standard: *Career Development and Occupational Studies: Standard 1*: Career Development

Resources: Newspapers, scissors, poster board, paper, glue, and markers

Lesson plan/procedure:

1. Divide class into groups of four.
2. Students will read a page or two of the newspaper looking for job titles. The team will cut and tape job titles on a big sheet.
3. The team will brainstorm a list of skills needed in each occupation and write that on the big sheet underneath each job title.
4. Dream up a first and last name for the person who has this job.
5. Then, all of the teams return to a large group and share their charts.
6. In going over the charts, ask for additional feed back from the rest of the class about the needed skills.

Evaluation:
Questions to ask the group:

-What are the reasons for choosing a male or female name for each job title?

-Are there jobs that only women can do?

-Are there jobs that only men can do?

Lesson 23: World of Work Spaceship

Name: Abby Hirsch

Grade Level: 6

National Standard: *Career Standard A*: Students will acquire the skills to investigate the world of work in relation to knowledge of self and to make informed career decisions.

NYS Standard:
Career Development and Occupational Studies: Standard 1: Career Development
Career Development and Occupational Studies: Standard 3a: Universal Foundation Skills

Lesson plan/procedure:
Describe the situation to the group of students. After reading the situation and the task, break the group into groups of eight to ten people if you are working with a larger class.

The Situation: A new planet has been found to support human life. It closely resembles earth. Scientists have found a safe way to transport a group of individuals to start a colony on the planet. The problem is that there are ten individuals volunteering to go and there is room for only seven.

The Task: You have been chosen to be a member of an impartial committee that is to decide which individuals will go to start the colony. Your group must decide based on the brief histories submitted by the interested individuals. Remember, your goal is to start a colony. Do not give gender of those not stated. This should be part of the discussion that follows.

Individuals:
1. Dancer 23 – Female
2. Scientist 42 – no family
3. Husband 33/ Wife 36 (Who is pregnant. Husband does construction work and is a craftsperson. Wife is a teacher. They will not be separated.)
4. Minister 63 – Male – A specialist in community relations
5. Police officer 35 – In good physical condition
6. TV News reporter 46 – Female

7. High school student interested in history – Male
8. Doctor (surgeon) – 58 Female
9. Computer programmer – 42 Male
10. Farmer – 29

Discussion: Have groups discuss their choices. Stress how they decided the gender or the scientist, police officer and farmer.

Evaluation: Students will demonstrate learning by participating in group discussion about their selections.

Lesson 24: Machines on Mars

Name: Nicole Lippitt

Grade Level: Sixth Grade

National Standard: *Career Standard A*: Students will acquire the skills to investigate the world of work in relation to knowledge of self and to make informed career decisions.

NYS Learning Standard:
Career Development and Occupational Studies: Standard 1: Career Development
English Language Arts Standard 4: Language for Social Interaction
The Arts Standard 2: Knowing and Using Arts Materials and Resources
Mathematics, Science, and Technology Standard 1: Analysis, Inquiry, and Design
Mathematics, Science, and Technology Standard 7: Interdisciplinary Problem Solving

Resources: Construction paper, markers, crayons, chalkboard (or marker board) and chalk

Lesson plan/procedure:

Counselor will assess students' level of understanding based on presentations and post-activity discussion.

Purpose:
1. To increase students' awareness of different occupations, including the importance of each.
2. To acquire effective skills for communicating with peers and adults.
3. To acquire skills necessary for working on a team.
4. To increase each student's ability to plan and make decisions.

Goals:
1. To have each team present on a career of their choice.

Procedure:
1. Ask students to imagine that a space shuttle will be sent to Mars, but that only machines can be sent to do the work.

2. Pair students up randomly and explain that each team will need to think of an occupation that should be sent on the shuttle. Each team will design a machine to do the work of that occupation on Mars.
3. Give students an example, such as a dentist machine with drills for arms and an x-ray machine as the body.
4. Ask students to draw the machines and to label all the parts. They should also make a list of the functions that each machine can perform.
5. Have each team present their machine to the class.
6. Following the presentations, generate a discussion with students about the activity. What makes each occupation important? What was it like to work as a team? Who made the decisions? Who drew the machine? Are there any drawbacks to using machines for these occupations?

Evaluation:
Increased awareness will be assessed through group discussion.

Adapted from:
Harvath, S. (1980). *Expanding your alternatives: Mission Venus. Curriculum ideas for Elementary school settings.*

Middle Level Activity Book

Lesson 25: Career Vision

Name: Judy Fruiterman

Grade Level: Sixth and Seventh Grades

National Standards:
Career Standard A: Students will acquire the skills to investigate the world of work in relation to knowledge of self and to make informed career decisions.
Career Standard B: Students will employ strategies to achieve future career goals with success and satisfaction.
Career Standard C: Students will understand the relationship between personal qualities, education, training, and the world of work

NYS Learning Standards:
English Language Arts Standard 1: Language for Information and Understanding
English Language Arts Standard 4: Language for Social Interaction
Career Development and Occupational Studies: Standard 1: Career Development

Resources: Beatle's song, "When I'm 64," Chart paper and magic markers
Lesson plan/procedure:

Pass out sheet with the words to the song "When I'm 64." Play the song while the students read the words. Have a discussion about the meaning of the song.

Pass out chart paper and markers. Have students project into the future and draw:
1. What they will look like when they are 34?
2. Where will they live?
3. What will their residence look like?
4. Who will they live with? Married? Single?
5. Will they go to college, military, or right to work after high school?
6. What will be their highest level of education?
7. What career will they have when they are 34?
8. What will be their approximate salary?
9. What hobbies will they have?
10. What kind of car will they drive?

This will take 15-20 minutes for students to think and draw all the elements of their imagined life. Then each student will show and explain his/her chart to the whole class. The counselor will tape all the charts around the room. A discussion will follow about the careers they have chosen. Will they have the appropriate education to achieve those careers?

Evaluation: Students will be able to discuss how their chosen career might affect the lifestyle they are envisioning.

Lesson 26: Ask a Neighbor!

Name: Bob Wilkins

Grade Level: 6

National Standard: *Career Standard A*: Students will acquire the skills to investigate the world of work in relation to knowledge of self and to make informed career decisions.

NYS Standard:
Career Development and Occupational Studies: Standard 1: Career Development
English Language Arts Standard 1: Language for Information and Understanding

Lesson plan/procedure:

Ask the group to interview several neighbors. In the interviews, the students will have the opportunity to ask neighbors about work. Some possible questions that they could ask would be:

1. Do you work outside or inside?
2. Do you have to do a lot of paperwork?
3. Do you spend a lot of time talking with people?
4. Did you choose your job because of the amount of pay or salary?
5. How much schooling did you need? Does someone today need the same amount of schooling?
6. Do you have to travel a lot in your job?
7. Do you have to live in a certain area to do your job?

Return the following week to allow students to report back on their interviews.

Evaluation:
Students will present their interviews to the class to demonstrate their learning.

New York State Comprehensive School Counseling Program

Lesson 27: Family Strength or Family Weakness?

Name: Christine McBrearty Hulse

Grade Level: 6

National Standard: *Personal/Social Standard A*: Students will acquire the knowledge, attitudes, and interpersonal skills to help them understand and respect self and others.

NYS Standards:
Career Development and Occupational Studies: Standard 3a: Universal Foundation Skills
Health, Physical Education, and Family and Consumer Sciences Standard 2: A Safe and Healthy Environment
English Language Arts Standard 1: Language for Information and Understanding

Lesson plan/procedure:

Use these questions as a means to generate discussion. After asking each person in the group to fill out the questionnaire, ask the group to discuss why they answered the questions as they did. The facilitator needs to be very sensitive to strong feelings that may be connected to some of the answers.
   A. Are there some families that get along better than others do?
   B. Why do some families do a better job than others do?

S = Strength W = Weakness

1. Eating meals together:

2. Individuality:

3. Freedom of feelings, thoughts, desires, fantasies:

4. Everyone has equal value:

5. Family members can be different:

6. Parents do what they say:

7. Atmosphere is fun:

8. Mistakes are forgiven:

9. Large family (more than four children):

10. Secrets:

11. Approval must be earned:

12. Unconditional love:

13. Ridged roles:

14. Perfectionism:

15. Competition:

16. Given choices:

17. Self love:

18. Trust:

19. Arguments:

20. Both parents working:

21. Ridged rules:

22. Flexible rules:

23. Family vacations:

24. Separate vacations:

25. No vacations:

26. Sharing housework:

List three strengths your families have:

1._____

2._____

3._____

Evaluation:
Students will demonstrate learning through worksheet and discussion.

Lesson 28: Who Am I?

Name: Bob Wilkins

Grade Level: 7

National Standard: *Personal/Social Standard A*: Students will acquire the knowledge, attitudes, and interpersonal skills to help them understand and respect self and others.

NYS Standards:
Career Development and Occupational Studies: Standard 1: Career Development
English Language Arts Standard 4: Language for Social Interaction

Resources: Blank note cards and markers

Lesson plan/procedure:

Tell the class that they are going to think about what makes each of them different from everyone else. Distribute the blank note cards. Then ask students to put three words on each note card that would describe them to other people. Then allow time for each person to think of three descriptive words for themselves.

Then, break the group into groups of three. Have each person in the triads tell the other two about why those words were chosen. After this is finished, ask the two other persons to agree or disagree with what the words say.

Evaluation:

Group Activity: Then ask the whole group to pull together. Have a group discussion and ask the following questions:

1. What did you learn about yourself during the exercise?

2. Did you learn anything about someone else that you did not know before?

New York State Comprehensive School Counseling Program

Lesson 29: How Do I Look?

Name: Christine McBrearty Hulse

Grade Level: 7

National Standard: *Personal/Social Standard A*: Student will acquire the knowledge, attitudes, and interpersonal skills to help them understand and respect self and others.

NYS Standards:
Career Development and Occupational Studies: Standard 1: Career Development
English Language Arts Standard 4: Language for Social Interaction

Resources: Black construction paper (24" by 18"), white newsprint, markers, film projector, copies of sheets titled "How I See Myself" and "This Is How Others See Me"

Lesson plan/procedure:

This is a long range activity. When the project is finished, the student will have several visual reminders showing how they see themselves and how others see them.

Week 1: Each student will complete the "How I See Myself" activity sheet (following page). Collect these when they are finished. While the students are completing the "How I See Myself" activity sheet, pull students one by one to have their silhouette traced. Place each young person in the light of a film projector to trace his or her silhouette on newsprint.

Week 2: Use the "How I See Myself" activity sheet to play the game "Who Is This?" Read each activity sheet and ask the students to guess the identity of the person. Then ask how they arrived at their guess.

Pass out the "How I See Me" activity sheet (following page). Tell the students that they need to have the people on the sheet fill out a comment about them. Tell the students that they have one week to ask the people to fill out the sheet.

Week 3: Use the "How Others See Me" activity sheet to play the game "Who Is This?" Read each activity sheet and have the students guess who the person is. Ask the guesser how they knew. Ask the person whose paper it is how they feel about what was written about them.

Evaluation:
Students will demonstrate their learning by displaying their finished project.

"How I See Myself"

If I were an animal, I would be:_____

Why:_____
_____

If I were an insect, I would be:_____

Why: _____

If I were a color, I would be:_____

Why: _____
_____

If I were a piece of food, I would be:_____

Why: _____
_____

This Is How Others See Me

Comments from:

A Parent: _____
_____
_____
_____

A Teacher: _____
_____
_____
_____

A Friend: _____
_____
_____
_____

A Classmate: _____
_____
_____
_____

New York State Comprehensive School Counseling Program

Lesson 30: Talk To Yourself

Name: Christine McBrearty Hulse

Grade Level: 7

National Standard: *Personal/Social Standard A*: Students will acquire knowledge, attitudes, and interpersonal skills to help them understand and respect self and others.

NYS Standards:
Career Development and Occupational Studies: Standard 2: Integrated Learning
English Language Arts Standard 4: Language for Social Interaction

Resources: Paper and pen

Lesson plan/procedure:

1. Discuss what a "put down" is (something that someone says that makes you feel badly about yourself).
2. Ask the students to think about three times that they frequently end up feeling nervous, uptight, or frightened (taking an exam, giving a speech, asking someone to go out with you, etc).
3. Ask the students to make a list of "put downs" that they tell themselves during tense moments ("I am so dumb," I cannot ever do anything right," I will probably make a mistake").
4. Then, have the students list helpful things that they could say to themselves instead of the put downs (I am going to do a good job of this," "I will give this my best shot").

Discussion:
Would anyone like to share some of his/her putdowns?
How can these putdowns make matters worse?
Would anyone like to share some helpful things to say instead of the putdowns?

The next time you find yourself in a situation where you feel nervous, frustrated or tense, do the following:

> **Stop putting yourself down.**
> **Take a few deep breaths.**
> **Tell yourself things about yourself. Reacting to tense situations by putting yourself down is a habit that you can break. <u>It will take some practice.</u>**

Evaluation:
Students will be able to articulate how their negative self-talk affects them.

New York State Comprehensive School Counseling Program

Lesson 31: Choose To Win!

Name: Ann Morrone

Grade Level: 7

National Standards:
Academic Standard A: Students will acquire the attitudes, knowledge, and skills that contribute to effective learning in school and across a lifespan.
Career Standard A: Students will acquire the skills to investigate the world of work in relation to knowledge of self and to make informed career decisions.
Personal/Social Standard A: Students will acquire the knowledge, attitudes, and interpersonal skills to help them understand and respect self and others.

NYS Standards:
Career Development and Occupational Studies: Standard 3a: Universal Foundation Skills
English Language Arts Standard 4: Language for Social Interaction

Resources: Paper and pencil to draw a logo and to write slogans. If available, gummed labels that can be worn

Lesson plan/procedure:

Begin by saying, "W have looked at people around us to learn the characteristics of winners and losers. We have also looked at ourselves to see where we are on the losers/winners scale and we have thought of activities we might do to try to move ourselves toward the winner's mark. When you come right down to it, though, whether we become winners or not depends more upon one thing than anything else. That one thing is our attitude. If we develop a good, positive attitude and learn that nothing will keep us from being a winner, then guess what? We will be winners!"

Divide the class into small groups. Each group creates a slogan to inspire one to work toward being a winner. They also may draw a logo and display the slogan around this logo as a button to be worn. After completion, one member from each group presents their button to the class and explains its meaning and how the group decided upon it.

Summary:

"In this unit we have looked at winners and losers. The title of our activity was "Choose to Win." We hope you have come away with the idea that whether you become a winner or a loser is mainly up to you. With a good attitude and a good effort, you too, can "Choose to Win!"

Evaluation: We have come up with several very clever and inspiring slogans. How are they alike? How are they different? How can a slogan be useful in helping us reach a goal?

New York State Comprehensive School Counseling Program

Lesson 32: What is the Healthy Choice?

Name: Shari Forth

Grade Level: 7

National Standards:
Career Standard A: Students will acquire the skills to investigate the world of work in relation to knowledge of self and to make informed career choices.
Personal/Social Standard B: Students will make decisions, set goals, and take necessary action to achieve goals.
Personal/Social Standard C: Students will understand safety and survival skills

NYS Standards:
Career Development and Occupational Studies: Standard 2: Integrated Learning
Health, Physical Education, and Family and Consumer Sciences Standard 1: Personal Health and Fitness
The Arts Standard 1: Creating, Performing, and Participating in the Arts

Resources: Worksheet entitled "Problem Solving," ideas for role-play

Lesson plan/procedure:

1. Ask students to recap what they learned last year about stress (definition of stress, ways to identify stress, ways they deal with stress).
2. Explain that, often, our inability to make healthy and effective choices is what causes stress.
3. Hand out sheet entitled "Problem Solving."
4. Review the steps with the class.
5. Take out the ideas for role-play. Ask for volunteers to role-play sample difficult situations. Explain that, by using the steps of problem solving, difficult situations can be less stressful.
6. As each group role-plays their situation, have the other students act as observers, noting what was healthy and effective.

7. Following each role-play, ask the observers to give feedback to the actors. Eventually, include the entire class in the discussion of the situations.
8. Summarize the lesson by reviewing the steps of problem – solving. Emphasize that, although they will not

Suggestions for Role – Plays:

1. Your adult neighbor called and asked if you could do some yard work for him. You are not doing anything now, but you are waiting for your best friend to call to firm up some plans you had made.
2. Your parents want you to go to church with them, and you would rather sleep in.
3. You know you are overweight, but it is so hard when all of your friends are eating junk food. They encourage you to enjoy the snacks with them.
4. You got into trouble with a teacher for talking. However, you are not the guilty person. It was your best friend who was talking. Your teacher's mistake put you on detention.

Evaluation:
Students will demonstrate their learning through various role – plays.

Problem – Solving:

1. Identify the problem.

2. Brainstorm all possible solutions. Write a list, if you can.

3. Think about the consequences of each possible solution. Ask yourself: "What could happen if I did this?"

4. Choose the best solution.

5. Do it!

Lesson 33: Dear Gabby

Name: Shari Forth

Grade Level: 7

National Standards:
Career Standard A: Students will acquire the skills to investigate the world of work in relation to knowledge of self and to make informed career decisions.
Personal/Social Standard B: Students will make decisions, set goals, and take necessary action to achieve goals.
Personal/Social Standard C: Students will understand safety and survival skills.

NYS Standards:
Career Development and Occupational Studies: Standard 3a: Universal Foundation Skills
Health, Physical Education, and Family and Consumer Sciences Standard 3: Resource Management

Resources: Students will need paper and a pen or pencil, chalkboard and/or overhead, chalk/marker

Lesson plan/procedure:

1. Remind students that we continually face difficult issues.
2. We have two ways of dealing with them: in a healthy way, or in a not – so – healthy way.
3. Have the students take out a sheet of paper and a pen or pencil.
4. Instruct them to write a letter to "Dear Gabby" about a physical, personal, or social problem they are having.
5. Remind them that no names are to be used in this exercise. Explain that the letters will be completely anonymous.
6. Collect the papers when the class is finished writing.
7. Select one or two papers to read to the class.
8. Ask the class how they would answer if they were Gabby.
9. Ask them to focus on a possible healthy solution to the problem?

10. At the end of the session, reemphasize that even with tough situations, there are several ways of dealing with them. Encourage students to use their problem solving steps, and other healthy ways of dealing with tough situations.

Note: Another way this could be done is by having the teacher write the letters and have the students respond individually, then in group discussion.

Evaluation:
Students will demonstrate learning through group discussion questions.

Lesson 34: How Are Other People Different?

Name: Abby Hirsch

Grade Level: 7

National Standard: *Personal/Social Standard A*: Students will acquire knowledge, attitudes, and interpersonal skills to help them understand and respect self and others.

NYS Standards:
Career Development and Occupational Studies: Standard 2: Integrated Learning
English Language Arts Standard 1: Language for Information and Understanding

Lesson plan/procedure:

Select five members of the group who have special differences. Be sure to contact them ahead of time to ask for their willingness to participate. Another possible approach is to ask for volunteers from the group. State, "For this exercise, I will need the help of five people who have some differences that may be obvious and some that may not be obvious." Have each of the five people tell his/her difference in one sentence.

Examples:
- I am Spanish.
- I am Cuban.
- I am from Iraq.
- I am Jewish.
- I come from a single parent family.
- I am a latchkey kid.
- My parents never went to college.
- My parents have doctoral degrees.
- I am left-handed.
- I am in special education.
- My parents come from another country.
- I am an only child.

- I get help with my reading.

As each person speaks, have the group write the first five descriptive responses that occur to them. Example: I am a latchkey kid.

Five Impressions:
- Neglected
- Lonely
- Undisciplined
- Too much responsibility
- Sad

Following the written impressions about all five people, ask for sharing of these impressions and responses from the individual involved. Discuss the causes of prejudices, the harm done, and ways to break down the walls of misunderstanding.

Ask what we do in school that helps dispute these prejudices (such as guidance lessons, social studies, etc.).

Evaluation:
Student will demonstrate learning by participating in discussion of prejudices.

Lesson 35: What Does It Take?

Name: Robert Wilkins

Grade Level: 7

National Standards:
Academic Standard B: Students will complete school with the academic preparation essential to choose from a wide range of substantial postsecondary options, including college.
Personal/Social Standard C: Student will understand safety and survival skills.

NYS Standards:
Career Development and Occupational Studies: Standard 3a: Universal Foundation Skills
Social Studies Standard 5: Civics, Citizenship, and Government
The Arts Standard 2: Knowing and Using Arts Materials and Resources

Resources: Poster board, markers, magazines (optional), scissors, paste

Lesson plan/procedure:

Begin by saying, "Everyone says that we need to be good citizens. What does this mean? What does it take to be a citizen in a democracy like the United States? Sometimes we talk about things like good citizenship, yet people may have different ideas about what that idea means. All of us can be, or will be, a part of what our country becomes. The country will become what the citizens make of it. What do you believe a good citizen does? What do you believe a good citizen looks like?"

Divide the class into small groups. Give each group a poster board, markers, and magazines (optional). "Your task today is to make a group poster on your ideas about what good citizens look or act like. This poster could include words and pictures that will describe the good citizen." Allow groups to work on posters for approximately 20 minutes. Have the groups present posters to the entire class.

Evaluation:
"What are some things that were similar about the posters? What was different? It is interesting and important to know about others' ideas that may be different from our own. Perhaps, the one common thread would be willingness to support the democratic process. The continuation of democracy will involve a degree of effort by the citizens of that democracy."

Middle Level Activity Book

Lesson 36: Qualities of Citizenship

Name: Robert Wilkins

Grade Level: 7

National Standards:
Academic Standard B: Students will complete school with the academic preparation essential to choose from a wide range of substantial postsecondary options, including college.
Personal/Social Standard C: Students will understand safety and survival skills.

NYS Standards:
Career Development and Occupational Studies: Standard 3a: Universal Foundation Skills
Social Studies Standard 5: Civics, Citizenship, and Government

Resources: Worksheet titled "Qualities of Citizenship"

Note: This lesson takes two sessions.

Lesson plan/procedure:

Before the session, make copies of the attached worksheet. After distributing one sheet to each person, discuss what it takes to be a citizen. "What does it take to be a citizen?" Do we possess those qualities?

Look at the worksheet. Take the sheet with you and think about it during your day. As you go through the day, think about the qualities and whether you exhibit those qualities. As you think about these qualities, so you think these qualities are needed to be a good citizen?

During the next session, ask people how they did on the worksheet. Do they believe that they possess the qualities? Based on how they act everyday, do they act as shown? Ask for discussion about why the qualities would be needed to be a good citizen.

Evaluation:
Allow time for discussion since there will be some differences of opinion. Stress the ways that people can tell whether they have the qualities.

New York State Comprehensive School Counseling Program

Qualities of Citizenship

Look at the list of qualities in the left column. Think to yourself whether you possess these personal qualities. Indicate your answer on the sheet. Then think about whether these qualities are needed to be a good citizen. Put your answer in the right column.

Personal Quality	**Is This Me? Yes/No**	**Needed to be a citizen?**
Dependable		
Being on time to meetings		
Organized		
A team "player"		
Writes well		
Speaks well		
Takes initiative		
Completes tasks on time		

Regular attendance		
Listens when people talk		
Can accept criticism		
Learns new things		

Lesson 37: I Need A Compliment; How About You?

Name: Christine McBrearty Hulse

Grade Level: 7

National Standard: *Academic Standard A*: Students will acquire the attitudes, knowledge, and skills that contribute to effective learning in school and across the life span.

NYS Standards:
Career Development and Occupational Studies: Standard 1: Career Development
English Language Arts Standard 4: Language for Social Interaction

Lesson plan/procedure:

Column 1: List five things you feel you do well.

Column 2: Name a person who told you so.

Column 1	Column 2
1. _____	1. _____
2. _____	2. _____
3. _____	3. _____
4. _____	4. _____
5. _____	5. _____

Complete the Following:

1. What are two feelings you have when you give someone a compliment?

   _____ and _____

2. Why might someone feel embarrassed when they are given a compliment?

   _____ and _____

3. How do want others to react when you compliment them?

   _____

4. How often do you compliment others?

   A friend_____
   Mom or Dad_____
   A favorite classmate_____
   A teacher_____
   A classmate you do not like so well_____

5. How important might compliments be to:

	Very Important	Somewhat Important	Not so Important
Your best friend	_____	_____	_____
Your mom and/or dad	_____	_____	_____
A classmate with few friends	_____	_____	_____
An older person living next door to you	_____	_____	_____

Procedure:
- Distribute copies of the sheet to each student.
- Instruct the students to complete column 1 an 2.
- Ask students to share their responses.

Next, ask students if compliments are really necessary. Usually from this point, and after sharing responses from column 1 and 2, students are so eager to share that the remainder of the page sometimes becomes more like a discussion guide, than a written exercise.

Evaluation:
Students will demonstrate their learning by keeping a list of compliments they have given or received throughout the week.

Lesson 38: The Spider Web

Name: Christine McBrearty Hulse

Grade Level: 7

National Standard: *Personal/Social Standard A*: Students will acquire the knowledge, attitudes, and interpersonal skills to help them understand and respect self and others.

NYS Standards:
Career Development and Occupational Studies: Standard 1: Career Development
English Language Arts Standard 4: Language for Social Interaction

Resources: Skein of black yarn, chairs in a circle

Lesson plan/procedure:

Give the skein of yarn to someone and ask that they introduce themselves and answer a simple question such as: What do you enjoy doing? What is your favorite food? State something that you consider one of your greatest accomplishments.

The first person holds onto the yarn and pitches the skein to another participant who introduces himself/herself and then reintroduces the preceding person. The activity continues until all participants have had a chance to introduce themselves and to reintroduce someone else.

The result of this activity is that an intricate web of black yarn is created as everyone learns one another's name and vital information. After the last person is introduced, the spider web can be "unspun" by working in reverse.
As a variation, one teacher in the building used white yarn to produce a winter "snowflake."

NOTE: This activity not only serves to help acquaint everyone in a newly formed group, but also provides for an excellent photo opportunity.

Evaluation:
Students will demonstrate learning by repeating the information of the previous people before introducing themselves.

Lesson 39: More Than a Label

Name: Abby Hirsch

Grade Level: 7

National Standard: *Personal/Social Standard A*: Students will acquire the knowledge, attitudes, and interpersonal skills to help them understand and respect self and others.

NYS Standards:
Career Development and Occupational Studies: Standard 1: Career Development
English Language Arts Standard 4: Language for Social Interaction

Resources: Note cards with labels and attached string so the cards can be used as headbands

Lesson plan/procedure:

Ask for eight volunteers. Tell the class that you are going to put headbands on the volunteers. The class should not tell the volunteers what the headbands say. Select headbands at random and fasten the headbands so that the labels are on the volunteers' foreheads. The headbands should have messages like the following:

1. I AM A NERD! Call me a nerd!
2. I AM POPULAR! Praise me.
3. I AM ALWAYS WRONG! Disagree with whatever I say.
4. I AM NOT SMART! Call me "Stupid!"
5. I AM AN OUTCAST! Ignore me.
6. I AM ALWAYS RIGHT! Agree with me.
7. I AM FUNNY! Laugh at me.
8. I AM BEAUTIFUL! Compliment me.

Group Task: Then, the group should stand in a circle and do what the headbands say. After about ten minutes, have the group stop. Ask the volunteers the following questions:
1. What do you think your sign said?
2. What did you like/dislike about the treatment?

Evaluation:

Have the volunteers join the rest of the class. Then have a discussion about what it is like to be labeled. Ask for examples (without names) where people have been labeled.

Lesson 40: Good or Bad Choices?

Name: Bob Wilkins

Grade Level: 7

National Standard: *Personal/Social Standard B*: Students will make decisions, set goals, and take necessary action to achieve goals.

NYS Standards:
Career Development and Occupational Studies: Standard 3a: Universal Foundation Skills
Health, Physical Education, and Family and Consumer Sciences Standard 3: Resource Management

Resources: Paper, pencils, chalkboard

Lesson plan/procedure:

1. Ask each person in the larger group to make two columns like below:

    "Good Choices"   "Bad Choices"

2. Then, ask them to spend a few minutes to think of times when they have made good choices. Good choices would lead to a positive result. After some time, ask them to think of several times when they made bad choices. Bad choices would lead to a negative consequence.

3. Then ask each person to think about his or her good and bad choices. With the successful choices, would they be inclined to make those same choices again? If so, why? If not, why?

    With the choices that led to bad results, would they make the same choices? If yes, why? If no, why?

4. Finally, ask the larger group if there were any surprises by doing this activity. Ask if anyone wishes to share his/her experience. Why would this person choose as they would now in the same circumstances?

Evaluation:
Students will demonstrate learning by discussing and giving examples of good and bad choices.

Lesson 41: Are My Skills Useful?

Name: Bob Wilkins

Grade Level: 7

National Standards: *Career Standard A*: Students will acquire the skills to investigate the world of work in relation to knowledge of self and to make informed career decisions.

NYS Standards:
Career Development and Occupational Studies: Standard 3a: Universal Foundation Skills
Health, Physical Education, Family and Consumer Sciences Standard 3: Resource Management

Resources: "Are My Skills Useful?" Worksheet

Lesson plan/procedure:

1. To prepare for the session, the counselor should make copies of the attached worksheet. Distribute the worksheets to the group. Ask each person to think first about some areas where they have some skills and interest. Ask them to list these in the left column of the worksheet.

2. After the group has had some time to think about this. Ask people to share some of their answers. Allow some time for people to talk. The time will allow for some further thought about individual skills that may not have been considered.

3. Then, ask the group to think of where they might use the skill in school. Give a little time for this thought. Ask volunteers to share some of their answers. Once again, allow some time for this so that ideas may be shared.

4. Finally, ask the group to think about how they might use the skills in the community. After several minutes, ask volunteers to share their answers. As ideas are shared, some participants will realize that school is just part of the larger community. Useful skills at school will also be useful in the larger community.

Evaluation:

For closure, ask participants to share any new understandings with the larger group. Some of the group will recognize some new talents, while others will see new uses for talents already recognized.

Are My Skills Useful?

Sometimes we undermine the value of our skills and interests. Please list the things you like to do and feel that you have some skill. Then, think about those places where you could use the skill and interest at either school or in the community.

Interest and Skill	Possible Use at School	Possible Use in the Community

New York State Comprehensive School Counseling Program

Lesson 42: The Ring of Names!

Name: Bob Wilkins

Grade Level: 7

National Standards:
Career Standard A: Students will acquire the skills to investigate the world of work in relation to knowledge of self and to make informed career decisions.
Personal/Social Standard A: Students will acquire the knowledge, attitudes, and interpersonal skills to help them understand and respect self and others.

NYS Standards:
Career Development and Occupational Studies: Standard 1: Career Development
English Language Arts Standard 4: Language for Social Interaction

Note: This is a good beginning of the year activity for building relationships.
Lesson plan/procedure:

1. Have students sit or stands in a circle. Tell them that you want them to think of **ONE** word that starts with the same letter as their first name <u>**that describes who they are.**</u> Then start with yourself and introduce yourself to the person on your left by saying that word and your first name.

    Example: Hello, I am "Rapid Robert!"

2. Then ask the person on your left to introduce himself/herself in the same way and to introduce you using your word and your first name.

    Example: Hello, I am "Sophisticated Sharie." This is "Rapid Robert!"

3. Continue around the circle with each person introducing himself or herself in the same way and then introducing ALL of the people who were already introduced.

CLOSURE: Once everyone has been introduced, people will have a lot of fun. In addition, they will have explored the relationship between repetition and association to help with learning. Tell them, "Today, you have learned a bunch of new names. By repeating these names over and over, you found that this was one help. In addition, you learned that it helped to connect or associate the names with a meaningful word. Not only was the activity useful to learn names, but other things as well. You might try this idea when you need to learn a list of names or other facts."

Evaluation: Students will demonstrate learning by being able to introduce everyone in the group.

New York State Comprehensive School Counseling Program

Lesson 43: The Five W's

Name: Bob Wilkins

Grade Level: 7

National Standards:
Academic Standard A: Students will acquire the attitudes, knowledge, and skills that contribute to effective learning in school and across a lifespan.
Academic Standard B: Students will complete school with the academic preparation essential to choose from a wide range of substantial postsecondary options, including college.
Career Standard B: Students will employ strategies to achieve future career goals with success and satisfaction.

NYS Standards:
Career Development and Occupational Studies: Standard 3a: Universal Foundation Skills
English Language Arts Standard 1: Language for information and Understanding

Resources: Several History passages from a Social Studies book or several passages from a sample of literature, chalkboard, paper, pencils

Lesson plan/procedure:

Tell the group that they are going to learn to listen for important things to study. List the five "W's" on the chalkboard (who, what, when, where and why). Define what each means. Tell the group that you want each person to listen for these things as they listen to a passage being read.

Read a passage that contains a description of an event. Ask the group to listen and to record the five "W's" that apply to the passage. After reading the passage, ask volunteers to tell what they think each "W" happens to be. List the correct answers on the board.

Tell the group that if they listen for these five "W's" then they will sort out what is important either reading or listening. Tell them that it is important to know the five "W's" of any event or reading or class activity when preparing for a test. Then ask the group to read another passage quietly to themselves and to list the five "W's" on the piece of paper. Ask for volunteers to share their answers then record these answers on the board.

Emphasize that people will improve their ability to prepare for tests by listening for the five "W's." Check back with the group in several weeks to review successes using the technique.

Evaluation:
Students will demonstrate learning by volunteering answers to the group discussion.

New York State Comprehensive School Counseling Program

Lesson 44: Why People Like What They Do

Name: Shari Forth

Grade Level: 7

National Standards:
Career Standard A: Students will acquire the skills to investigate the world of work in relation to knowledge of self and to make informed career decisions.
Career Standard C: Students will understand the relationship between personal qualities, education, training, and the world of work.
Personal/Social Standard A: Students will acquire the knowledge, attitudes, and interpersonal skills to help them understand and respect self and others.

NYS Standards:
Career Development and Occupational Studies: Standard 1: Career Development
Career Development and Occupational Studies: Standard 2: Integrated Learning
Career Development and Occupational Studies: Standard 3b: Career Majors

Lesson plan/procedure:

1. Have students select two adults to interview.

   Sample interview questions could be:

   - What are some of your interests?

   - How/why, did you become interested in each thing?

   - What special abilities do you need to do these things of interest?

2. Point out relationships between interests and abilities.

Evaluation:
Following the interviews, discuss the results with the students. Let students draw conclusions based on their data.

New York State Comprehensive School Counseling Program

Lesson 45: Out With the Old – In With the New

Name: Judith Fruiterman and Judith Karis

Grade Level: 7

National Standards:
Career Standard A: Student will acquire the skills to investigate the world of work in relation to knowledge of self and to make informed career decisions.
Career Standard B: Students will employ strategies to achieve future career goals with success and satisfaction.
Career Standard C: Students will understand the relationship between personal qualities, education, training, and the world of work.

NYS Standards:
Career Development and Occupational Studies: Standard 1: Career Development
Career Development and Occupational Studies: Standard 2: Integrated Learning
Career Development and Occupational Studies: Standard 3b: Career Majors

Resources: Advertising flyers, catalogues, poster board, markers

Lesson plan/procedure:
Break the larger group into smaller groups of five. Ask each group to list household items that were not in existence sixty years ago. Distribute advertising flyers and catalogues. Have each group give their examples and create a list. Due to new household items, list jobs that were created because of these items. Also, list jobs that were eliminated because of the new items.

Have students create a poster board displaying the new jobs.

Example: **The ice industry:** jobs eliminated - cutters, deliverymen, etc…
The refrigeration industry: jobs created – mechanics, electrical engineers, steel manufacturers, etc…

Is there a gender connected with the various jobs? List the gender of the people who typically did these jobs that were eliminated. List the gender of the people who typically do the jobs that were created. What does that tell us about the changing workforce?
Discuss how technology and society changes the nature of jobs and may create new jobs or eliminate others. Link the discussion to the fact that new jobs need more skills.

Ask the students to think of a job described in a writing of science fiction. What jobs would that fictional machine eliminate? What jobs would be created?

Evaluation: Students will demonstrate learning by displaying their poster boards.

New York State Comprehensive School Counseling Program

Lesson 46: Male or Female?

Name: Bob Wilkins

Grade Level: 7

National Standards:
Career Standard A: Students will acquire the skills to investigate the world of work in relation to knowledge of self and to make informed career decisions.
Career Standard B: Students will employ strategies to achieve future career goals with success and satisfaction.

NYS Standards:
Career Development and Occupational Studies: Standard 1: Career Development
Career Development and Occupational Studies: Standard 2: Integrated Learning
Math, Science and Technology Standard 5: Technology

Resources: Paper, pencils, chalkboard

Lesson plan/procedure:

Ask the students to list what they believe are "Male" career. Next, ask the class to list what they think are "Female" careers. Ask a few volunteers to read their lists aloud to the rest of the class. Then, ask the group if they agree with the gender assigned to each career. Ask for a majority vote where there is some disagreement whether a career is "Male" or "Female."

Break the larger group into groups of four. Assign each group at least four choices from the list on the chalkboard. Tell the groups that each group must research the "Male" and "Female" careers by using the Internet and career books provided. The groups are to write descriptions of each career in terms of required training and physical requirements.

In the next session, ask the groups to present the results of the research. As the group describes a "Male" or "Female" career, make certain that the description clearly outlines the physical requirements and the amount of training. Then ask the class whether the training or physical requirements would keep a member from the other sex from pursuing that career.

Evaluation:
After the presentations, ask the class to discuss why they think various careers are considered "Male" or "Female." Remind the class that they do not need to limit their career choices based on labels attached to certain careers.

New York State Comprehensive School Counseling Program

Lesson 47: What's In a Name?

Name: Bob Wilkins

Grade Level: 7

National Standards:
Career Standard A: Students will acquire the skills to investigate the world of work in relation to knowledge of self and to make informed career decisions.
Career Standard B: Students will employ strategies to achieve future career goals with success and satisfaction.

NYS Standards:
Career Development and Occupational Studies: Standard 1: Career Development
Career Development and Occupational Studies: Standard 2: Integrated Learning
Career Development and Occupational Studies: Standard 3b: Career Majors

Resources: Paper, pencils, chalkboard, "The List" (attached)

Lesson plan/procedure:

Distribute the list of careers (following page) to the class. Ask the class to look at the list and decide whether the careers are limited to certain types of people. Ask the class to think about the list as you provide the following categories of people:

1. Young people
2. Older people
3. "Jocks"
4. Males
5. Females
6. "Smart" people

Evaluation:
After the class has assigned categories to all the careers, ask volunteers to discuss why they assigned the categories the way that they did. Ask the class to think about the physical requirements for a particular career. Also, ask the class to think about how much training is needed for each career. Due to the training or physical requirements, would some people be excludes from that career? If not, why have we assigned these careers to certain types of people?

The List

ACCOUNTANT
ARCHITECT
ASTRONAUT
BASEBALL PLAYER
BASKETBALL PLAYER
BOOKKEEPING
CHEMIST
CHORUS LEADER
COMPUTER TECHNICIAN
ELEMENTARY TEACHER
ENGINEER
MARINE BIOLOGIST
MARINE INFANTRY
MATHEMATICIAN
MUSICIAN
PILOT
PROFESSIONAL SINGER
PSYCHOLOGIST
RACE CARE DRIVER
SAILOR
SCHOOL COUNSELOR
SOLDIER
SURGEON
VETERINARIAN
ZOOLOGIST

Lesson 48: I Am Unique – What Makes Me Special?

Name: Abby Hirsch

Grade Level: 8

National Standards: *Personal/Social Standard A*: Students will acquire the knowledge, attitudes, and interpersonal skills to help them understand and respect self and others.

NYS Standards:
Career Development and Occupational Studies: Standard 1: Career Development
English Language Arts Standard 4: Language for Social Interaction

Resources: "What Makes Me Special?" worksheet

Lesson plan/procedure:

Before the session, make copies of the attached worksheet: "What Makes Me Special?" Gather the group, and tell the class that they are going to think about what makes each of them special and unique. Then, distribute the worksheet and allow time for each person to answer all the questions.

Allow some time for thought about the questions. Then, have a group discussion and ask volunteers to share their answers.

Evaluation:

Some questions to ask could be:

In question one, was it easy to think of words to describe yourself?
What did people say about the second question? What do people think has been an important factor in who we are? Do people think their parents have been important? Relatives? Friends?

New York State Comprehensive School Counseling Program

What about question number three, was it difficult to think of an accomplishment? How about our greatest accomplishment?

In terms of question four, was this difficult? If you had difficulty with this question, could or would you be willing to ask your friend/s over the next several days?

In question number five, what were their answers? Do you think this answer might be different at a different time in your life?

Middle Level Activity Book

What Makes Me Special?

Instructions: Before you begin to think about what makes you unique, please THINK about and ANSWER the following questions/ Write down you initial impressions or thoughts. It is important to be honest in your answers.

1. Write three positive words that describe you.

    (1.)_____ (2.)_____ (3.)_____

2. What single factor contributes most to who you are as a person?

    _____

    _____

3. What do you consider your greatest accomplishment?

    _____

    _____

4. What would your best friend describe is you most positive attribute?

    _____

    _____

5. What would you most like to be remembered for in your life?

    _____

    _____

New York State Comprehensive School Counseling Program

Lesson 49: Your Personality Strengths

Name: Abby Hirsch

Grade: 8

National Standard: *Personal/Social Standard A*: Students will acquire the knowledge, attitudes, and interpersonal skills to help them understand and respect self and others.

NYS Standards:
Career Development and Occupational Studies: Standard 1: Career Development
English Language Arts Standard 4: Language For Social Interaction

Resources: "Where Is Your Personality" worksheet

Lesson plan/procedure:

Tell the group that they are going to think about their positive qualities and strengths. Distribute the worksheet and ask the students to circle those words that best describe their personal qualities. Allow time for the group to work on the sheet.

Evaluation:
After the group is finished, ask them the following questions:

1. Did you learn anything new about yourself because of the activity?
2. Are there more positive qualities than you realized?
3. How might you use the qualities that you have, in ways that you have not in the past?

Where Is Your Personality?

Take a moment to think about your personality characteristics. These personal qualities make you special and unique. Not everyone takes the time to think about what makes him or her special.

Instructions: Circle words that describe who you are. Think about words that you use to describe yourself. Think about your viewpoint, your personality, your character, intellect, and outlook. Be as objective as possible.

Active	Enthusiastic	Professional
Adventurous	Expressive	Quick
Affectionate	Faithful	Rational
Alluring	Friendly	Realistic
Ambitious	Gentle	Receptive
Approving	Genuine	Reassuring
Aspiring	Good	Responsive
Ardent	Graceful	Self – aware
Articulate	Guarded	Sensible
Assertive	Humorous	Sensitive
Attractive	Happy	Serious
Busy	Honest	Sincere
Brisk	Industrious	Skillful
Caring	Insightful	Sociable
Charismatic	Involved	Spontaneous
Confident	Kind	Steady
Congenial	Knowing	Stimulating
Conscientious	Logical	Strong
Considerate	Likable	Supportive
Cooperative	Open – minded	Talented
Creative	Optimistic	Talkative
Dependable	Objective	Tolerant
Determined	Organized	Trusting
Disciplined	Orderly	Truthful
Distinctive	Original	Visionary
Dynamic	Outgoing	Witty
Eager	Patient	
Efficient	Pensive	
Empathetic	Persistent	
Engaged	Poised	
Energetic	Precise	
Enterprising	Productive	

Lesson 50: Feelings Are Okay!

Name: Charles Todd

Grade: 8

National Standard: *Personal/Social Standard A*: Students will acquire the knowledge, attitudes, and interpersonal skills to help them understand and respect self and others.

NYS Standards:
Career Development and Occupational Studies: Standard 1: Career Development
English Language Arts Standard 1: Language for Information and Understanding

Resources: Pencils and "Dealing with Feelings" worksheet

Lesson plan/procedure:

Explain that the focus of the lesson is that feelings are okay, both negative and positive ones. It is how we act that is important. We will be learning healthy ways to deal with feelings.

Also, discuss the relationship between feelings and self – esteem. Discuss that there will be highs and lows and that the media tells us it is okay to have "bad" feelings. Ask for examples.

Ask the students for examples of healthy ways of dealing with feelings.

Give the students steps for dealing with feelings in a healthy way:
1. Take time to feel the feeling.
2. Ask what is causing the feeling.
3. Choose healthy ways to manage feelings.
4. Have students complete "Dealing with Feelings" worksheet.

Evaluation:
Have students write a written response on these three questions:
(Lesson Continued)

1. How does the way you deal with feelings affect the way you see yourself (i.e. self esteem)?
2. What are the ways you usually deal with your feelings?
3. What are your most common feelings?

Ask students to share what they have written.

Dealing with Feelings

What are the ways that you deal with feelings? Here are some ideas. Circle the ones that you have tried.

Go shopping	Go to a movie	Sit in the sun
Play guitar, drums, etc.	Read a book	Take a walk
Watch T.V.	Ask for help	Play a sport
Talk to a teacher or counselor	Listen to music	Talk with a friend
Call someone on the phone	Punch a pillow	Clean your room
Run around the block	Ride a bike	Work on a hobby
Talk with an adult or parent	Paint or draw	Write a letter
Write in a journal	Write a story	

Directions: Using the list above or your own ideas, list at least two ways of dealing with each of the following feelings:

Anger: Loneliness or Rejection:

_____   _____

_____   _____

Sadness or Unhappiness: Boredom or Restlessness:

_____   _____

_____   _____

Lesson 51: Different Places – Feeling Different

Name: Robert Wilkins

Grade: 8

National Standards:
Personal/Social Standard A: Students will acquire the knowledge, attitudes, and interpersonal skills to help them understand and respect self and others;
Personal/Social Standard B: Students will make decisions, set goals, and take necessary action to achieve goals.

NYS Standards:
Career Development and Occupational Studies: Standard 1: Career Development
English Language Arts Standard 1: Language for Information and Understanding

Resources: Pencils, and "Feelings about Where We Are" worksheet

Lesson plan/procedure:

Distribute the attached worksheet to the group. Explain that we each feel differently in different situations or locations. Some of us will feel comfortable meeting new people. Others will feel very uncomfortable in the same situation.

Tell the group to picture themselves in the situation or location listed on the worksheet. Ask them not to spend a lot of time thinking about each situation before recording a feeling. Tell them to write the first feeling that comes to mind. Let the group know that they will not have to share their feelings if they choose not to. Allow the group time to think about their answers.

Evaluation:
Ask the group these questions when they are finished:
1. Were there any "Right" or "Wrong" answers to the situations?
2. Is it okay to feel afraid, uncomfortable or any other feeling in these situations?
3. Because of your feelings, do you avoid any of these situations or circumstances?
4. Are there any "wrong" feelings that you might feel?

Feelings about Where We Are

Think about being in these different situations or places. How would you feel? Remember to give the first feeling or feelings that come to mind. Do not spend time being concerned with "Right" or "Wrong" answers.

Situation: **Feeling/s:**

Writing an essay   _____

Talking with a teacher   _____

Calling someone on the phone   _____

Talking with a parent   _____

Writing in a journal   _____

Going shopping   _____

Reading a book   _____

Asking for help from a friend   _____

Asking for help from a stranger   _____

Punching a pillow   _____

Hugging a teddy bear   _____

Meeting someone for the first time   _____

Meeting someone you know   _____

New York State Comprehensive School Counseling Program

Lesson 52: Pressure

Name: Shari Forth

Grade: 8

National Standard: *Personal/Social Standard A*: Students will acquire the knowledge, attitudes, and interpersonal skills to help them understand and respect self and others.

NYS Standards:
Career Development and Occupational Studies: Standard 1: Career Development
English Language Arts Standard 1: Language for Information and Understanding
Health, Physical Education, and Family and Consumer Sciences Standards 1: Personal Health and Fitness:
Health, Physical Education, and Family and Consumer Sciences Standards 2: Safe and Healthy Environment

Resources: Chalkboard, chalk, index cards, pen/pencil

Note: This is a two-part activity.

Lesson plan/procedure:

Lead the class in a discussion on pressure. What is it? Where does it come from? How do you know you are experiencing it? How do you deal with it? (Make sure that peer pressure is a major part of this discussion.)
1. Write the words "Physical," "Social," and "Emotional" on the chalkboard.
2. Distribute index cards.
3. Have the students write at least on pressure they currently face, or have they recently faced. Emphasize that the cards will be anonymous.
4. Collect the cards.
5. Explain that by using the cards, the pressures that the class has written will be discussed.
6. Read the pressures listed on the cards, then ask the class whether the problem is physical, social, or emotional.
7. How many other students have been in a similar situation? How did they deal with it?

8. Have students interview someone they respect about a time when that person faced a difficult situation.

Evaluation:
At the end of the period, ask the students to summarize what they have learned from the lesson.

New York State Comprehensive School Counseling Program

Lesson 53: Real Life Situations

Name: Shari Forth

Grade: 8

National Standard: *Personal/Social Standard A*: Students will acquire the knowledge, attitudes, and interpersonal skills to help them understand and respect self and others.

NYS Standards:
Career Development and Occupational Studies: Standard 1: Career Development
English Language Arts Standard 1: Language for Information and Understanding
Health, Physical Education, and Family and Consumer Sciences Standards 1: Personal Health and Fitness:
Health, Physical Education, and Family and Consumer Sciences Standards 2: A Safe and Healthy Environment
Math, Science and Technology Standard 5: Technology

Resources: Results of interviews from last session, newspapers, magazines, Internet resources

Lesson plan/procedure:

1. Have one or two students review the highlights of the last session.
2. Ask students to take out the results of their interviews.
3. Ask for volunteers to share what they have found.
4. Discuss how the students handled the situation. How would they have handled it? Do they think the person handled it appropriately? Were they surprised by the person's decision?
5. Using the newspapers, magazines, and Internet resources, ask the student to find examples of real life situations in which people are faced with the difficult physical, social, and emotional challenges.
6. Divide the students into work groups. Each group should select one issue that would be relevant to people in their age level.

Evaluation:
The group should examine and discuss the way the situation is or was handled, and how they think it should have been handled, and why. If it was handled well, explain why. At the end of the class, explain that life is made up of choices. Each choice we make can be made healthily or unhealthily. It is important for each of us to examine ALL of our options before deciding on a course of action.

NOTE: It would be especially good if some of the articles dealt with the current day "Idols" and their decisions.

New York State Comprehensive School Counseling Program

Lesson 54: Are these Good Things?

Name: Robert Wilkins

Grade: 8

National Standard: *Personal /Social Standard A*: Students will acquire the knowledge, attitudes, and interpersonal skills to help them understand and respect self and others.

NYS Standards:
Career Development and Occupational Studies: Standard 2: Integrated Learning
English Language Arts Standard 4: Language For Social Interaction

Resources: Chalkboard, paper, pens or pencils

Lesson plan/procedure:

Before the session, make copies of the attached sheet. Once the group is settled, distribute the worksheets. Tell the group that they will be listening to one another. While they are listening to one another, they should be thinking about things that make the other people in the group either the same or different from themselves. They should focus on the positive qualities of the other person.

First, ask the group to write down on a piece of paper some things that they do well. Then, tell them that they can use the sheets of paper to help them when they talk. Ask each person to briefly describe who he or she is. Ask them to talk about a number of things that they do well.

Instruct the group to listen carefully for the things that the person says that they do well. Then, ask them to think about whether they share this skill. Ask them to record the items on the attached sheet.

Evaluation:

After everyone has had a chance to speak, ask volunteers to share what they heard about other people in the group. Ask them to share the skills that make the person the same or different from himself or herself.

As volunteers speak, make sure that people speak with respect about the other person, even when they are talking about things that are different.

The Same Skills?

As the person tells about himself or herself, write down at least three skills they possess that make them the same as you. Also, write down at least three skills that you do not have.

Example:	The Same:	Different:
Charlie Brown	Reads well	Good at football
	Knows about computers	Can make pizza
	Does well at math	Spells well

Person's Name:	The Same:	Different:
A.	1.	1.
	2.	2.
	3.	3.
B.	1.	1.
	2.	2.
	3.	3.
C.	1.	1.
	2.	2.
	3.	3.
D.	1.	1.
	2.	2.
	3.	3.
E.	1.	1.
	2.	2.
	3.	3.
F.	1.	1.
	2.	2.
	3.	3.

Middle Level Activity Book

G.   1.   1.
        2.   2.
        3.   3.

H.   1.   1.
        2.   2.
        3.   3.

I.   1.   1.
        2.   2.
        3.   3.

New York State Comprehensive School Counseling Program

Lesson 55: I See Some Good Things!

Name: Robert Wilkins

Grade: 8

National Standards: *Personal /Social Standard A*: Students will acquire the knowledge, attitudes, and interpersonal skills to help them understand and respect self and others.

NYS Standards:
Career Development and Occupational Studies: Standard 2: Integrated Learning
English Language Arts Standard 4: Language For Social Interaction

Resources: "The Good Things!" worksheet, pencils

Lesson plan/procedure:

Before the session, the leader should make copies of the attached sheet. Say, "Today, we are going to think about qualities of people who are both the same and different from ourselves."

Part One: Picture someone who is different from you. See if you can think of some positive qualities of that individual. List these positive qualities on the worksheet. You will not have to share what you have listed on the worksheet unless you choose to. You will also not have to say whom you were thinking about. You may wish to say something to the person later. If you can, think of positive qualities that are different from your own positive qualities.

Part Two: Now, find out if you can think of some positive qualities that belong to you. List these on the worksheet. You will not have to share these.

Evaluation:
Some questions to ask:
Was it difficult to think of positive qualities of the person who is different?
Was it difficult to think of positive qualities that apply to you?
Were there some qualities that you have in common?
Do you have more qualities in common, than you would have thought before this exercise?

The Good Things!

First, think about someone that is different from you. You will not need to share what you put on this activity sheet. Think about some positive qualities of that person. List these positive qualities. Then think about yourself. List some positive qualities that you possess.

A Person Who Is Different:	**Someone Like Me:**
Positive Quality:	Positive Quality:
Positive Quality:	Positive Quality:
Positive Quality:	Positive Quality:
Positive Quality:	Positive Quality:
Positive Quality:	Positive Quality:
Positive Quality:	Positive Quality:
Positive Quality:	Positive Quality:

New York State Comprehensive School Counseling Program

Lesson 56: Helping A Friend

Name: Anne Morrone

Grade: 8

National Standards: *Personal /Social Standard A*: Students will acquire the knowledge, attitudes, and interpersonal skills to help them understand and respect self and others

NYS Standards:
Career Development and Occupational Studies: Standard 1: Career Development
English Language Arts Standard 4: Language for Social Interaction

Resources: Paper, pencil, overhead projector or chalkboard

Lesson plan/procedure:

In this activity, students will identify strategies for helping a friend. Divide the class into small groups. Choose a recorder and a reporter for each group. Using the situations, say, "Your group's task is to brainstorm what the behaviors might mean if you observed a friend acting this way. Also, describe some things you could do to help your friend." Have each group report their suggestions. As the group leader reviews the suggestions, ask the group how many times the ideas listed in "What a Friend Can Do" were suggested.

Some examples of your friend's behavior:

Seldom smiles or laughs
Withdrawal from normal social contact
Reduces involvement in sports and games
Grades take a sudden drop
Procrastinates

Eats alone, Studies alone
Avoids groups
Drab dress
Sighs often and cries easily

What Can A Friend Do?

Listen, listen, and listen. Get your friend to talk to you. Talk to the person. Ask the person how he/she feels. If there does not seem to be a solution, suggest help from an adult.

If the person seems severely depressed, realize that your friend needs help from his/her parents, guardians, the school counselor, a teacher, or other adult that you trust.

Evaluation:
Students will demonstrate learning by participating in the group discussion.

New York State Comprehensive School Counseling Program

Lesson 57: What Would I Choose?

Name: Robert Wilkins

Grade: 8

National Standards:
Academic Standard A: Students will acquire the attitudes, knowledge, and skills that contribute to effective learning in school and across a lifespan.
Personal /Social Standard A: Students will acquire the knowledge, attitudes, and interpersonal skills to help them understand and respect self and others
Personal/Social Standard B: Students will make decisions, set goals, and take necessary action to achieve goals.

NYS Standards:
Career Development and Occupational Studies: Standard 2: Integrated Learning
English Language Arts Standard 4: Language for Social Interaction
Math, Science and Technology Standard 5: Technology

Resources: Paper, pencils, chalkboard, Internet resources

Lesson plan/procedure:
Ask the group to take out paper and a pencil. Ask them to write the following on the top of their paper: "Things I Know A Lot About." Then, ask them to think of some things that they know about and ask them to list these under the title. Allot about ten minutes for this.
Then, ask the group to take out a second sheet of paper. Ask them to write the following at the top of the paper: "Things I Do Not Know Much About." Direct them to think of the things they do not know much about and to list these on this sheet of paper. Allot about ten minutes for this.

Conduct a class discussion about whether people will feel comfortable trying things on the first list. People will say that they would feel more comfortable trying these activities when familiarity is involved. Ask the group how might they feel about doing things that involve the activities on the second sheet. Stress that they are less likely to try these things, than the things they know.

Finally, ask the group how they might find out about some things on the second list. Have them brainstorm all the ways they could gather information about these things. As they think of ideas, list them on the chalkboard. Ask them whether they might be more likely to try some of these things if they found more information about them.

Evaluation: Have students locate information on one item from their list of "Things I Know A Lot About" and from the list "Things I Do Not Know A Lot About" and research these items using the Internet. Students must supply a list of new facts regarding these two items.

New York State Comprehensive School Counseling Program

Lesson 58: What Is In My Future at High School – Part One

Name: Bob Wilkins

Grade: 8

National Standards: *Academic Standard B*: Students will complete school with the academic preparation essential to choose from a wide range of substantial postsecondary options, including college.

NYS Standards:
Career Development and Occupational Studies: Standard 1: Career Development
English Language Arts Standard 1: Language for Information and Understanding

Resources: Copies of the high school curriculum book, overlays showing a brief overview of the graduation requirements, an appointment book, overhead projector and screen

Note: This is a two-part lesson.

Lesson plan/procedure:

In this activity, there will be a group presentation where there is an overview of graduation requirements. Counselors should make certain that the overhead and the screen is in place before the group discussion. Counselors should also bring enough copies of the high school curriculum book for each student.

Using overlays of graduation requirements, the counselor should review the requirements for graduation. After a quick presentation, the counselor should turn off the projector. The counselor should have a quick game seeing how many students remember key facts. Some examples of game concerns would be: the number of years of English required, the number of courses required for mathematics and science, or whether physical education is required. Distribute the high school curriculum books. Briefly show some highlights of how to gain information using the book.

Evaluation: At the end of the session, tell the students that they can help make individual counseling sessions flow more smoothly. Ask the students to think of when they have open time such as a study hall. Ask the students to write their name under that day of the week and period of the day. For instance, the student would say that second period on Tuesdays would be good because that is when she or he has a study hall.

New York State Comprehensive School Counseling Program

Lesson 59: What Is My Future at High School – Part Two

Name: Bob Wilkins

Grade: 8

National Standards: *Academic Standard B*: Students will complete school with the academic preparation essential to choose from a wide range of substantial postsecondary options, including college.

NYS Standards:
Career Development and Occupational Studies: Standard 1: Career Development
English Language Arts Standard 1: Language for Information and Understanding
Math, Science and Technology Standard 5: Technology

Resources: High school curriculum book, brief overview of graduation requirements, four – year plan sheet, career and college material available if needed, students past years grade reports and achievement test results, internet resources

Lesson plan/procedure:

In the previous activity, there was a group presentation where there was an overview of graduation requirements. In this activity, the counselor should sit with the individual student and discuss options and plans.

Using the four-year plan sheet, the student should make plans for the four years of high school. Some choices are automatic since there are some mandated courses for all four years. Some choices must fit somewhere in the four year plan. Examples would be the two years of mathematics and science, the one-year of music or art, and the three years of language other than English.

This is a good time to connect dreams for the future with plans in the present. To varying degrees, the counselor may need to use achievement scores and past report cards. If the student has questions about preparation for a particular future career, career information should be readily available. In addition, this activity may lead to an interest in further exploration of college information. Therefore, access to college information is important and the Internet is a great resource.

Evaluation:
Counselor will evaluate student's progress by documenting students intended career path and goals.

New York State Comprehensive School Counseling Program

Lesson 60: A Time Plan!

Name: Bob Wilkins

Grade: 8

National Standards:
Academic Standard A: Students will acquire the attitudes, knowledge, and skills that contribute to effective learning in school and across a lifespan.
Personal/Social Standard B: Students will make decisions, set goals, and take necessary action to achieve goals.

NYS Standards:
Career Development and Occupational Studies: Standard 2: Integrated Learning
Health, Physical Education, and Family and Consumer Sciences Standard 3: Resource Management

Resources: Paper, pencils, chalkboard, computer

Lesson plan/procedure:

Tell the group that they are going to do some thinking about how best to use their time. One advantage of doing such a time study will be that they will also know hoe much time can be for leisure. For a take home assignment, ask each member of the group to approximate how much time should be spent on each subject from school. Ask each person to figure how much time is used for dinner and other things like practice, etc. Have students develop their weekly schedule on a computer or word processor.

On the next day, ask for volunteers. Ask several volunteers to show on the board how they allotted time during the evening. Once several examples are on the board, ask for discussion about whether these time plans would work for everyone. There will be many different opinions about the amount of time needed for various activities.

Ask if anyone is willing to do an experiment. Once there are several volunteers, ask these people if they would be willing to stick to their time schedule for one week.

Evaluation:
At the end of the week, ask for a report back from the volunteers. See if there was any change in academic satisfaction or performance. Most likely, there will be positive results to illustrate the value of time management.

New York State Comprehensive School Counseling Program

Lesson 61: I Didn't Know That!

Name: Shari Forth

Grade: 8

National Standards:
Career Standard A: Students will acquire the skills to investigate the world of work in relation to knowledge of self and to make informed career decisions.
Career Standard B: Students will employ strategies to achieve future career goals with success and satisfaction.
Career Standard C: Students will understand the relationship between personal qualities, education, training, and world of work.

NYS Standards:
Career Development and Occupational Studies: Standard 1: Career Development
Career Development and Occupational Studies: Standard 3b: Career Majors
Math, Science and Technology Standard 5: Technology

Note: You will need to give students a due date to complete assignments.

Resources: Computers and career books

Lesson plan/procedure:

1. Explain to the class that their goal, in this activity, is to find out what they do not know about a particular career.
2. Each student chooses an occupation to explore.
3. Using the library, Internet, career resources, Department of Labor, interviews, and other pertinent resources, the students are to research the skills and interests needed to pursue their occupational choice.

Evaluation:
When the class reconvenes, each student should share the occupation they researched, where their data originated, the skills and interests needed, and one skill that they were surprised to find related to that occupation.

Lesson 62: Part One – Our Town

Name: Shari Forth

Grade: 8

National Standards:
Career Standard A: Students will acquire the skills to investigate the world of work in relation to knowledge of self and to make informed career decisions.
Career Standard B: Students will employ strategies to achieve future career goals with success and satisfaction.

NYS Standards:
Career Development and Occupational Studies: Standard 1: Career Development
Career Development and Occupational Studies: Standard 2: Integrated Learning
Career Development and Occupational Studies: Standard 3b: Career Majors
Math, Science and Technology Standard 5: Technology

Resources: Drawing tools, long roll of white paper, Internet resources, and career materials

Note: This is a two-part lesson.

Lesson plan/procedure:

1. Have students make a drawing of their town. This is a group mural.
2. Ask students where people work in their town.
3. Discuss what they think each job entails, (duties, responsibilities, training, etc.)
4. Are there any jobs that would be considered "non – traditional?"
5. Break the larger group into several smaller groups. Ask each smaller group to research a particular "non traditional" career. They should research a job description, find out about working conditions, the skills needed, and type and amount of training needed.

Evaluation:
Have the students report back about their findings to the larger group.

New York State Comprehensive School Counseling Program

Lesson 63: Part Two – Our Town

Name: Shari Forth

Grade: 8

National Standards:
Career Standard A: Students will acquire the skills to investigate the world of work in relation to knowledge of self and to make informed career decisions.
Career Standard B: Students will employ strategies to achieve future career goals with success and satisfaction.

NYS Standards:
Career Development and Occupational Studies: Standard 1: Career Development
Career Development and Occupational Studies: Standard 2: Integrated Learning
Math, Science and Technology Standard 5: Technology

Resources: Drawing tools, long roll of white paper, Internet resources, and career materials

Note: This lesson would require further coordination of career visitors.

Lesson plan/procedure:

1. Have students write letters to several of the places of work listed in Part – One "Our Town." In the letters, they should invite someone to come to the class to speak about a non - traditional career found in the community.
2. Ask the visitor to describe their duties, training, skills, and positive or not so positive parts of the job.
3. Students may ask questions previewed by the teacher.
4. After each speaker, ask the students to share something new that they learned.

Evaluation:
The class should write thank you letters to each visitor. In each letter, students should be encouraged to cite something new that they learned.

Lesson 64: New and Futuristic Careers

Name: Judith Fruiterman and Judith Karis

Grade: 8

National Standards:
Career Standard A: Students will acquire the skills to investigate the world of work in relation to knowledge of self and to make informed career decisions.
Career Standard B: Students will employ strategies to achieve future career goals with success and satisfaction.

NYS Standards:
Career Development and Occupational Studies: Standard 1: Career Development
Career Development and Occupational Studies: Standard 2: Integrated Learning
Career Development and Occupational Studies: Standard 3b: Career Majors
Math, Science and Technology Standard 5: Technology

Resources: Poster boards, marker, Internet, and career resources

Lesson plan/procedure:

Futurists have identified several innovative career areas for the 21st century. These unusual occupations will not generate loads of jobs, but those who go into them will be doing things very different from people in the past.

Read the list: Choose two careers that would interest you and answer the following questions using the Internet and career resources:
1. How does this career relate to your interests and values?
2. What skills would be necessary for this career?
3. Describe your work environment for this career.
4. List another career that you think will be in your future.
   - Bionic Medical Technician
   - Underwater Archaeologist
   - Water Quality Specialist

- Retirement Counselor
- Vacation or Free – Time Consultant
- Electronic Mail Technician
- Pollution Botanist

Evaluation:
Have students report to the large group their findings on those new and futuristic careers.

Lesson 65: Changes in the World of Work

Name: Judith Fruiterman and Judith Karis

Grade: 8

National Standards: *Career Standard A*: Students will acquire the skills to investigate the world of work in relation to knowledge of self and to make informed career decisions.

NYS Standards:
Career Development and Occupational Studies: Standard 1: Career Development
Career Development and Occupational Studies: Standard 2: Integrated Learning

Resources: Magazine and newspaper articles on changes in the workforce (sample article on next page). **Note:** These must be located well before the lesson, with enough copies for each group.

Lesson plan/procedure:

Our economy and world economy are constantly changing. Sixty percent of you will be in jobs that do not exist today. No one knows what those jobs will be. We do know that you will need skills in reading, writing, math, and science.

Divide class into teams. Give each team an article that has implications relating to changes in the workforce.

Then, answer the following questions:

1. How will the events affect work and jobs?
2. How can workers prepare for the changes described?
3. What jobs might be eliminated?
4. What jobs might be created?

Evaluation:
Students will demonstrate learning by reporting answers to the group.

Lesson 66: A Business Visitation

Name: Ann Morrone, Richard Natoli & Kathy Stratton

Grade: 8

National Standards: *Career Standard A*: Students will acquire the skills to investigate the world of work in relation to knowledge of self and to make informed career decisions.

NYS Standards:
Career Development and Occupational Studies: Standard 1: Career Development
Career Development and Occupational Studies: Standard 2: Integrated Learning

Resources: Local businesses, buses, access to meeting room at home school, "Business Choice Sheet," "Planned Schedule for the Day," "Visitation Sheets"

Lesson plan/procedure:

In this activity, students will choose from a list of cooperating local businesses (using the "Student Services Business Visitation Sign – Up Sheet"). Then, the coordinator/s will need to collate groups for the business visits (see sample "Career Trip Schedule).

On the morning selected for the business visits, the students will make the trips on buses and tour the businesses. They will have the "Eighth Grade Career Visitation Sheet" to help formulate their questions. After the tour, the students will return to the home school.

Evaluation:
Once back at the home school, the bus groups will go to different meeting rooms. Once in the meeting rooms, the students will discuss the questions on the "Career Visitation Sheet." Ask the students if they learned anything new in this career visitation.

Middle Level Activity Book

Student Services Business Visitation Sign – Up Sheet

Date

Please fill in your name each time with your business choice

Student Name: _____ **Homeroom:** _____

Business First Choice: Write name of business from below _____

_____

Student Name: _____ **Homeroom:** _____

Business Second Choice: Write name of business from below

_____

Student Name: _____ **Homeroom:** _____

Business Third Choice: Write name of business from below

_____

Please choose three of the following in order of preference. If you choose the * choices, you will be going to both businesses.

**Note to potential users – Totally fictional names:

Pete's Fitness Club and Daycare Center – Health, Physical Fitness, Childcare
*Tuna and Family – Sales, Designer, Driver
Wide World Travel – Travel Agent, Office Worker, Computer Skills
City Highway Dept.: Equipment Operator, Laborer, Driver, and Government
The "Super Ad" Paper – Writer, Artist, Salesperson, Communications
Tammy's Sign Studio – Sign Painting, Computer Skills, Artist
*Department of Labor – How to find jobs, Clerical, Computer Skills
Honest Mary's Motors – Sales, Mechanic, Manager, Office Worker
WKRP Radio – Communication, Sales
*Tom's Inn – Food Services
"U Charge Em" Battery Service – Sales, Driver, Buyer

Accurate Tool and Die – Business Ownership, Machine Tool Maker
Local Post Office – Federal Government Work, Clerical, Computer Skills
Legible Printing Company – Advertising, Typesetting, Clerical
"Big Room" Hotel – Hotel Management, Receptionist

Middle Level Activity Book

Eighth Grade Career Visitation Sheet

Date:

Name:

Homeroom:

1. What business area did you visit?

2. What is their main product or function?

3. What is one major area of importance the employer stressed?

4. Are the jobs in this field increasing, staying the same or declining?

5. Has the trip increased your interest in this career/field?

6. How did this businessperson get involved in this career?

7. Is there a connection between this career and any education courses? What is the connection?

8. Explain one thing you learned as a result of this career visit.

9. Would you be interested in learning more about this career?

10. How would you rate the career visitation? Please explain.

New York State Comprehensive School Counseling Program

Lesson 67: Understanding Stress Feelings

Name: Ellen S. Bieber

Grade: 5-8

National Standards: *Pesonal/Social Standard C:* Students will understand safety and survival skills.

NYS Standard: *Health, Physical Education, and Family Consumer Sciences – Standard 2*: A Safe and Healthy Environment: Students will acquire the knowledge and ability necessary to create and maintain a safe and healthy environment.

Resources: "My Feelings" worksheet, "Three Things to Reduce My Stress" worksheet, pens or pencils

Lesson Plan:
As students enter the classroom, hand out "My Feelings" worksheet, to be completed silently and independently. When students have completed the sheet, share and discuss items # 1-5. Continue the discussion asking students to identify what stress is. What does stress feel like? Is stress good or bad? Discuss examples of different stresses. Have students share their own experiences, as they are comfortable. How do people with stress? (Discuss both: effective / healthy ways and ineffective / unhealthy ways).

Activity # 1: Birthday Order Game. Break the class into 2 groups and tell them they are being timed. Tell the students they may not use ANY verbal communication, or written communication. Instruct the students that they must line themselves up in chronological birthday order, beginning with January 1 and running in order until December 31. The group that does it accurately first "wins."
Afterwards, debrief. How did they complete the activity? What was frustrating? How did they overcome difficulties? What would have made it easier?

Activity #2: Alphabetized Order Game. Break the class into 2 groups. Ask each group to get in line alphabetically by first name. They may talk. There will be no winner. Debrief. How did they complete the activity? Was it challenging? Was it interesting / fun? Did they feel nervous or stress this time? Why/why not? Compare activities 1 & 2 to each other. What made the 1st one stressful, and the 2nd one not?

Closing Activity: Practice Relaxation. Have students sit back down. Lead them through relaxation exercises, including: closed eyes, slow, deep breathing, systematically relaxing each part of body, thinking calm thoughts, stretching. Afterwards, distribute "Understanding and Relieving Stress" worksheet as post-test.

Evaluation: Post-test using "Understanding and Dealing With Stress" worksheet

New York State Comprehensive School Counseling Program

My Feelings

1. I am happy when: _____

2. I feel angry when: _____

3. I feel sad when: _____

4. I feel nervous when: _____

5. I am clam when: _____

An example of when I feel pressure, anxiety, strain, constant worry, tension, or stress:

_____

_____

_____

An example of how I deal with feelings of stress is: _____

_____

_____

_____

Understanding and Reducing Stress

What is stress? _____

_____

_____

Three effective things I can do when I feel stressed out:

1. _____

2. _____

3. _____

Lesson 68: Tolerance and Anti-bias: Role Identity

Name: Ellen S. Bieber

Grades: 5 - 8

National Standard:
Personal / Social Standard A: Students will acquire the knowledge, attitudes, and interpersonal skills to help them understand and respect self and others.

NYS Learning Standard:
English Language Arts Standard 1: Language for Information and Understanding.

Resources:
Sufficient open classroom Space
"Person Cluster" worksheet for each student
A pen or pencil for each student, extra paper
A flipchart and marker or blackboard and chalk

Lesson Plan / Procedure:

Explain the rationale for this exercise. Hand out the Person Cluster worksheet. Instruct students to put their names in the center and fill out the other 5 circles with 5 groups with which they identify. Encourage participants to choose groups that represent who and what they are. Some examples might be religion, race, ethnic or cultural identification, gender, hobby/activity, family, friend, volunteer activity, language spoken, music or other arts, health / fitness, personality descriptor like caring, optimistic, stressed out, sensitive. Let the students know that there aren't any correct or wrong answers, and that since there are only 5 spaces, that on a different day they might choose 5 different groups to write in.

After students have completed the worksheet, have them break into small groups of 3 or 4 students. Ask 1 person from each small group to create a list of all the identifiers that students have listed in their molecules. No personal names should appear on the group's list. Collect all lists from the small groups.

Next, ask each student to choose 1 circle that is a primary source of identification. Don't say, "the most," just one that is primary and central. Have the students discuss this in their small group. Why was this their primary identifier? Ask them to discuss the positive and negative aspects of being connected to the one identifier they listed as primary.

As the students continue to discuss, write the small groups' lists on the blackboard or flipchart. Only list each group once.

When the small groups have completed their discussions, conduct a "stand-up." Call out several identifiers from the master list, one at a time, and ask people to stand up, take a quick look around, and then sit down. For example, " Stand up if you would describe yourself as a…" Be sure to call out the items that appeared on a few different lists, as well as others that might not be as common.

Large group discussion: Ask if anyone learned anything about him or herself that was a surprise. Ask how it felt to be the only one standing, or almost alone. Ask how it feels to be part of a large group. Ask students what they can do to ensure everyone in the school can stand with pride and confidence.

Ask each student to flip over the Person Cluster sheet and write an example on the back, of how they can help everyone in the school to stand with pride and confidence.

Collect the worksheets.

Evaluation: Person Cluster worksheet, with written response of how each students can help others in the school to feel confident and proud to be who they are.

New York State Comprehensive School Counseling Program

PERSON CLUSTER

Directions: 1. Write your name in the body of the person (center)
               2. In the other circles (head, hands, and feet) write the names of 5 groups with which you identify.

For sharing: Choose 1 group (a primary identity for you) and answer the following questions:

1. Share a time when you have felt very proud to be a member of that group.
2. Share a painful experience resulting from membership in that group.

New York State Comprehensive School Counseling Program

Lesson 69: Terms of Tolerance and Anti-bias

Name: Ellen S. Bieber

Grades: 7-8

National Standard:
Personal / Social Standard A: Students will acquire the knowledge, attitudes, and interpersonal skills to help them understand and respect self and others.

NYS Learning Standard:
English Language Arts Standard 1: Language for Information and Understanding.

Resources:
Sufficient open classroom Space
"Definitions" sheet (copyright 2000, Anti-Defamation League) for each student. Contact Anti-Defamation League to obtain sheet.

Lesson Plan / Procedure:

Icebreaker Activity: "The sun shines brightly." Move desks out of area, to create an open space for students to make circle their chairs. Stand in the center to explain the rules. Rules: No pushing, no shoving, be careful of each other, etc. One person will stand in the middle and say, "The sun shines brightly for anyone who...." And that person finishes the sentence with something about him or herself like gender, a sport played, favorite color, wearing a particular item of clothing (khaki pants, jeans, a baseball hat), musical instrument played, etc. Any of the students who have that thing in common, will stand up and move to another chair. The person left in the middle starts the 2nd round and the game continues. People have to move at least 2 chairs away when they move. Play 1 round for practice. Being a woman I might start with, "The sun shines brightly for anyone who is a female." As the girls get up to move, I take one of their chairs. The girl left in the middle starts the next round with, "The sun shines brightly for..." Continue the game for several rounds, about 10 minutes.
Discussion: How did it feel to be in the middle? What if you were the only one to have to move for something? Did you learn anything about anyone else?

Distribute Definitions sheet. As a group have students read aloud, one at a time, each of the 10 vocabulary words and definitions. Review any questions, have students give examples.

Break students into small groups or pairs. Assign each small group the task of discussing one Part II word. Instruct them to come up with an example from real-life, a book, or TV when they witnessed one of the "isms." After giving each group several minutes to work, come back into the large group circle to present. Have 1 member from each group read the definition and another member tell the story of the example.

Use the presentation time for others to be able to comment, ask questions, and discuss how that makes them feel. What would they do differently in the situation?

Evaluation Method:
Students will use proper terminology during classroom discussions while of the general terms often associated with diversity awareness and anti-bias resources.

Students will be verbally able to explain and give examples of "isms."

New York State Comprehensive School Counseling Program

Lesson 70: Aim for Your Star

Name: Beth Porterfield

Grades: 5-8

National Standards:
Academic Development Standard A: Students will acquire the attitudes, knowledge, and skills that contribute to effective learning in school and across the life span.
Academic Development Standard B: Students will complete school with the academic preparation essential to choose from a wide range of substantial postsecondary options, including college.
Career Development Standard A: Students will acquire the skills to investigate the world of work in relation to knowledge of self and to make informed career decisions.
Personal/Social Development Standards A: Students will acquire the knowledge, attitudes, and interpersonal skills to help them understand and respect self and others.

NYS Standards:
English Language Arts Standard 1: Language for Information and Understanding
The Arts Standard 1: Creating, Performing, and Participating in the Arts
Career Development and Occupational Studies Standard 1: Career Development

Resources:
- System for dividing class into random groups of five participants each *(i.e., Johnson & Johnson Cooperative Cards, playing cards, etc.)*
- One cardstock, pre-cut star per group
- Markers, crayons, pens, pencils per group
- Fishing line or yarn

Lesson plan/procedure:
School counselor will lead a discussion about the importance of goal setting, the difference between short-term and long-term goals, and how someone should set goals:

How are goals and dreams different?

Why should we set goals?

Describe someone who sets goals for him/herself.

What happens when we don't set goals for ourselves?

Give an example of a short-tem goal.

Give an example of a long-term goal.

Name a successful person you believe set goals for him/herself. What do you think those goals were?

How can goal setting help you live a healthy life?

New York State Comprehensive School Counseling Program

The school counselor will divide students into random groups of five. Students will be encouraged to identify in small group discussion their individual **short-term goals** for the _____ *(school year, semester, counseling group, etc.)* Students will then discuss their individual **long-term goals** *(i.e., graduating, going to college, finding a career direction, etc.)* Students will discuss the desired outcomes/results of those goals. How will they know they have been successful? How will students know they have accomplished their goals?

One pre-cut, cardstock star will be distributed to each group of five students. Students will work as a group to decorate the middle of one side of the star to read "short-term goals" and the other side to read "long-term goals." On the side decorated **short-term goals**, each of the five students will write his/her short-term goal on one of the five points of the star as well as the intended result of this goal. On the side decorated **long-term goals**, each student will write his/her long-term goal and intended result on one of the five points of the star.

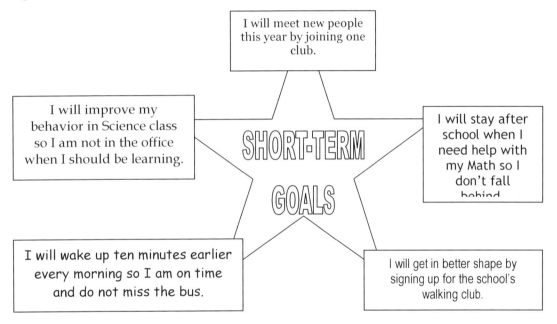

Students will apply their public speaking and listening skills by presenting their stars to the large group.

The counselor will conclude by reinforcing the importance of goal setting, discussing ways we can support each other with our goals, and encouraging students to believe in their dreams.

School counselor will hang the stars (by fishing line or yarn) so that the stars will serve as a visual reminder to students of the goals they set for themselves and the value of setting goals now and throughout a lifetime.

(*Location of stars (ceiling, doorway, bulletin board, etc.) should follow school procedures for displaying student work.)

Evaluation:
Students will understand the importance of setting goals.
Students will identify short-term and long-term goals and their intended results.
Students will recognize accomplished goals.
Students will apply communication skills *(active listening, verbal and nonverbal communication, public speaking, etc.)*
Students will produce a representation of their personal goals.

New York State Comprehensive School Counseling Program

Lesson 71: Career Zone

Name: Liza Leite and Griff Murray

Grade: 8

National Standards:
Academic Standard A: Students will acquire the attitudes, knowledge, and skills that contribute to effective learning in school and across the life span.
Career Standard A: Students will acquire the skills to investigate the world of work in relation to knowledge of self and to make informed decisions.

NYS Standards:
English Language Arts Standard 1: Language for Information and Understanding
Career Development and Occupational Studies Standard 1: Career Development

Resources:
1. Access to computer lab
2. Career Zone instruction sheet (see attached)

Lesson plan/procedure:
1. Pass out Career Zone instruction sheet
2. Have students log in to www.nycareerzone.org website
3. Create generic log in and password for students
4. Counselors review different career categories before students complete Interest Profiler
5. Students complete the 180 questions and read through their results

Evaluation: Each student will obtain a list of career choices. Students will be asked to read results and pick three careers that they are interested in. Students will write a summary of each of the careers that includes:
- Job Description
- Skills Necessary
- Education
- Salary

Students will share with classmates results found.

Middle Level Activity Book

CAREER ZONE WORKSHEET

Type: **www.nycareerzone.org**
Click on the first Career Zone to the left with flash site listed below it.

1. Read different categories.
2. Click on Assess Yourself: Read 6 interest areas.
3. My Portfolio
    a. Create an Account
        i. User Name:
        ii. Password:
        iii. Verify Password:
        iv. Password Reminder
        v. Fill in personal information
        vi. School:
        vii. Email address
        viii. Website address: use school's
        ix. Grade level:
    b. Save Your Work
4. Enter Career Zone
5. Click #2 My Interests
6. Start a new Interest Profiler
7. Click on each interest area and read definition
8. Click on View Occupations
9. Review your Interest Profiler

Lesson 72: Communication

Name: Kathy Postma

Grade: 6-8

National Standards:
Academic Standard A: Students will acquire the attitudes, knowledge, and skills that contribute to effective learning in school and across the life span.
Personal/Social Standard A: Students will acquire the knowledge, attitudes, and interpersonal skills to help them understand and respect self and others.

NYS Standards:
English Language Arts Standard 1: Language for Information and Understanding

Resources: Chairs to sit in specific formats for discussion with a classmate.

Lesson plan/procedure:
1. Pair off with another student. Place your chairs back to back and sit down. With your eyes open, talk with your partner about how you would spend $100.
2. Face your partner, stand toe to toe. Talk about what you would consider the perfect age.
3. Take two steps backward and try to communicate some message to your partner non-verbally. Do not talk!

Evaluation: Students will process the three activities with the following questions:
1. What differences do you notice in your behavior as you try to talk to your partner without being able to see him or her?
2. How do you feel about standing so close to your partner? How does facing him or her affect your communication?
3. How well do you think you communicated this time? How can you tell? What was being communicated by each of you?

Lesson 73: Equality

Name: Kathy Postma

Grade: 6-8

National Standards:
Academic Standard A: Students will acquire the attitudes, knowledge, and skills that contribute to effective learning in school and across the life span.
Personal/Social Standard A: Students will acquire the knowledge, attitudes, and interpersonal skills to help them understand and respect self and others.

NYS Standards:
English Language Arts Standard 1: Language for Information and Understanding

Resources: Paper and pencils

Lesson plan/procedure:
Ask students: "How is prejudice shown?"
    Examples: Using name calling; physical attacks; avoiding people
Ask students to identify examples of behavior under each of the categories identified and discuss the effect of each action.
    Examples: Individual acts of unfairness; institutional discrimination
After the discussion, on paper, have the students list groups of people who might be discriminated against.
    Examples: People from different ethnic groups; people who look different

Evaluation: Students will discuss the questions presented and write a personal account of discrimination that they may have seen or experience.

ASCA National Standards
Index to Lessons
The "Crosswalk"

Academic Development

Standard A: *Academic Standard A*: Students will acquire the attitudes, knowledge, and skills that contribute to effective learning in school and across the life span.

    Lesson numbers 1, 3, 4, 13, 16, 17, 19, 20, 21, 31, 37, 43, 57, 60, 61, 62, 63, 70, 71, 72

Standard B: Students will complete school with the academic preparation essential to choose from a wide range of substantial postsecondary options, including college.

    Lesson Numbers 35, 36, 43, 58, 59, 61, 62, 63, 70

Standard C: Students will understand the relationship of academics to the world of work, and to life at home and in the community

    Lesson number 61

Career Development

Standard A: Students will acquire the skills to investigate the world of work in relation to knowledge of self and to make informed career decisions

    Lesson numbers 10, 11, 22, 23, 24, 25, 26, 31, 32, 33, 41, 42, 44, 45, 46, 47, 64, 65, 66, 71

Standard B: Students will employ strategies to achieve future career goals with success and satisfaction.

    Lesson numbers 25, 43, 45, 46, 47, 64, 70

Standard C: Students will understand the relationship between personal qualities, education, training, and the world of work

    Lesson numbers 25, 44, 45

Personal Social Development

Standard A: **Students will acquire the knowledge, attitudes, and interpersonal skills to help them understand and respect self and others.**

> Lesson numbers 1, 2, 3, 4, 5, 9, 10, 11, 12, 14, 15, 18, 21, 27, 28, 29, 30, 31, 34, 38, 39, 42, 44, 48, 49, 50, 51, 52, 53, 54, 55, 56, 57, 68, 69, 70, 72

Standard B: **Students will make decisions, set goals, and take necessary action to achieve goals.**

> Lesson numbers 9, 13, 15, 16, 32, 33, 40, 51, 57, 60

Standard C: **Students will understand safety and survival skills.**

> Lesson numbers 6, 7, 8, 32, 33, 35, 36, 67

Legend: A:A-1. 1 = Academic Domain, Standard A, Competency I, and Indicator I.
Reprinted with permission from the American School Counselor Association

New York State Learning Standards
Index to Lessons

Health, Physical Education, and Family and Consumer Sciences
Standard 1: Personal Health and Fitness

    Lesson numbers 32, 52, 53

Health, Physical Education, and Family and Consumer Sciences
Standard 2: A Safe and Healthy Environment

    Lesson numbers 6, 7, 8, 27, 52, 53

Health, Physical Education, and Family and Consumer Sciences
Standard 3: Resource Management

    Lesson numbers 1, 11, 12, 13, 16, 19, 21, 33, 40, 41, 60

Mathematics, Science, and Technology
Standard 1: Analysis, Inquiry, and Design

    Lesson number 24

Mathematics, Science, and Technology
Standard 2: Information Systems

Mathematics, Science, and Technology
Standard 3: Mathematics

Mathematics, Science, and Technology
Standard 4: Science

Mathematics, Science, and Technology
Standard 5: Technology

    Lesson numbers 46, 53, 57, 59, 61, 62, 63, 64

Mathematics, Science, and Technology
Standard 6: Interconnectedness: Common Themes

    Lesson number 20

Mathematics, Science, and Technology
Standard 7: Interdisciplinary Problem Solving

    Lesson numbers 10, 24

English Language Arts
Standard 1: Language for Information and Understanding

    Lesson numbers 5, 14, 15, 18, 25, 26, 27, 34, 43, 50, 51, 52, 53, 58, 59, 68, 69, 70, 72

English Language Arts
Standard 2: Language for literary Response and Expression

English Language Arts
Standard 3: Language for Critical Analysis and Evaluation:

    Lesson number 17

English Language Arts
Standard 4: Language for Social Interaction:

    Lesson numbers 1, 3, 4, 5, 9, 14, 24, 25, 28, 29, 30, 31, 37, 38, 39, 42, 48, 49, 54, 55, 56, 57

Languages Other Than English
Standard 1: Communication Skills

Languages Other Than English
Standard 2: Cultural Understanding

The Arts
Standard 1: Creating, Performing, and Participating in the Arts

    Lesson numbers 14, 15, 32, 70

The Arts
Standard 2: Knowing and Using Art Materials and Resources

    Lesson numbers 24, 25, 35

The Arts
Standard 3: Responding to Analyzing Works of Art

The Arts
Standard 4: Understanding Cultural Contributions of the Arts

Career and Occupational Studies
Standard 1: Career Development

    Lesson numbers 1, 3, 4, 6, 7, 8, 12, 18, 22, 23, 24, 25, 26, 28, 29, 37, 38, 39, 42, 44, 45, 46, 47, 48, 49, 50, 51, 52, 53, 56, 58, 59, 61, 62, 63, 64, 65, 66, 71

Career and Occupational Studies
Standard 2: Integrated Learning

    Lesson numbers 9, 10, 13, 16, 19, 30, 32, 34, 44, 45, 46, 47, 54, 55, 57, 60, 62, 63, 64,

    65, 66

Career and Occupational Studies
Standard 3a: Universal Foundation Skills

    Lesson numbers 11, 17, 20, 21, 23, 27, 31, 33, 35, 36, 40, 41, 43

Career and Occupational Studies
Standard 3b: Career Majors

    Lesson numbers 44, 45, 47, 61, 62, 64

Social Studies
Standard 1: History of the United States and New York

Social Studies
Standard 2: World History

Social Studies
Standard 3: Geography

Social Studies
Standard 4: Economics

Social Studies
Standard 5: Civics, Citizenship, and Government
    Lesson numbers 35, 36

Made in the USA
Charleston, SC
25 October 2016